Unguarded Moments

For Jessi
Hope you learn a
few things, laugh
a lot & enjoy these
stories! Thanks for
doing the tour!

Langh

Unguarded Moments

Stories of Working Inside the Missouri State Penitentiary

LARRY E. NEAL & ANITA NEAL HARRISON

Truman State University Press
Kirksville, Missouri

Cover art: photo by Anita Neal Harrison

Cover design: Teresa Wheeler

Library of Congress Cataloging-in-Publication Data

Neal, Larry Edmund, 1951–
Unguarded moments : stories of working inside the Missouri State Penitentiary
/ Larry Neal & Anita Neal Harrison.
    pages cm
ISBN 978-1-61248-110-4 (alk. paper) — ISBN 978-1-61248-111-1 (ebook)
1. Neal, Larry Edmund, 1951– 2. Missouri State Penitentiary. 3. Prisons—
Missouri—Officials and employees—Biography. 4. Prisoners—Missouri.
I. Harrison, Anita Neal, 1981– II. Title.
HV9475.M82.M576 2014
365'.977855—dc23
[B]

                                                                    2014006626

The paper in this publication meets or exceeds the minimum requirements of
the American National Standard for Information Sciences—Permanence of
Paper for Printed Library Materials, ANSI Z39.48–1992.

To Diana Lynn, beloved wife and mother.

Contents

Illustrations

Foreword

For whatever reasons, the American public is intrigued by what lies behind the walls of our prisons. The old Missouri State Penitentiary (MSP) in Jefferson City is no exception.

Since its opening in 1836 until after its closing in 2004, there have been numerous publications about the historic prison. Works relating the MSP story have dealt with fact and fiction, the sensational, the macabre, and, since its closing, the paranormal. Most of the material written has focused on the negative aspects of confinement within the oldest prison west of the Mississippi River. Humor is infrequently addressed in the publications, most probably because of the misconception that no humor can be found in such places. Nothing is further from the truth.

In this book, Larry E. Neal, a former maintenance employee of the Missouri State Penitentiary and later chief engineer at the Jefferson City Correctional Center, gives the reader a rare inside view of prison humor as seen through his eyes and those of the individuals he worked with.

In previous publications on MSP, the exploits of notorious convicts and heroic correctional staff have been documented by street authors, as well as by former staff and both male and female offenders who served time there. The stories seldom related are those compiled by civilian employees like Neal.

Referred to as "square men," these civilian employees held the vast majority of positions within MSP, including caseworkers, teachers, nurses, doctors, plumbers, food service workers, electricians, and everything in between. These employees are often overlooked as being critical components in the daily operations of prisons the size of small cities.

At MSP, offender workers, both skilled and unskilled, often

received work assignments under prison civilian staff. A unique coexistence formed as a result. Long-term offenders might work with the same staff members for many years. Under such circumstances, it would be unreasonable to assume that some bonds did not develop between the keepers and the kept. Prison staff must assume responsibility to maintain and manage within the parameters of what is and is not permitted in such relationships. It is essential that public safety and institutional safety always be the highest priorities. A common misconception is that prison staff exist to punish offenders when, in fact, prison staff exist to ensure that offenders remain secure for whatever length of sentence the judicial system has imposed. Prison staff must recognize that offenders are human beings and that the vast majority of offenders will reenter society.

The opportunity to develop real relationships creates an opportunity for real fun and laughter, despite the less-than-ideal circumstances of a maximum-security prison. Although some of Neal's stories may seem far-fetched, his account of life within MSP is true. The author shows what took place beneath and above the forty-two acres of MSP. He takes the reader into the steam tunnels and attics of the massive nineteenth- and early twentieth-century structures that made up the MSP complex. Neal graphically illustrates the often filthy and dangerous conditions in which square men and convicts worked together to solve problems with potentially serious consequences.

In this book, Neal documents an era that has long since passed from the Missouri prison system. While many of his stories would today be possible grounds for offender and staff disciplinary action, his stories show that indeed there was laughter and humor within the MSP stone walls. Most significantly, in relating that humor, Neal draws attention to the common thread of humanity found in each of us.

> Mark S. Schreiber
> Deputy Warden (retired)
> MSP/JCCC

Acknowledgments

We owe our thanks to several people:

Peggy Miller, who read countless drafts, made improvements, and told us we could do this. Thanks for the editing and, even more, for the encouragement.

Mark Schreiber, who answered MSP history questions, allowed us free use of his photo collection, and read the manuscript to ensure our facts were straight. Thanks, Spanky, for your generosity.

Charles Reineke and Mary Barile, who helped us connect with the Truman State University Press. Thanks for the tip!

L. G. Patterson, who dug through his files to find the final image in this book. Thanks for the favor.

The team at Truman State University Press, who helped two first-time book authors realize a dream. Thanks for your professionalism.

Our family, who supported us in this endeavor and in so many others. Thanks for your love.

The MSP staff and inmates, who helped write this book with their parts in the MSP story, and especially my friend Ed Hanauer, who is guilty of everything I say about him in this book. Thanks, everyone, for the memories.

And, finally, Diana Neal (1953–2011), whose love still inspires us. We thank God for you.

Prologue
The Way It Really Was

He was six feet and 350 pounds. He was naked, he was a convict, and he was hollering threats of revenge.

I was a little nervous.

But my coworker was laughing, and he was the one Gritter* was coming after.

I had just started working in the Missouri State Penitentiary plumbing shop, and Gritter was one of the convicts assigned to work for me. A big old country boy, he didn't normally go streaking. He was exiting the shower and had just picked up his undershorts when, from around the corner, my coworker Richard Baumann appeared with a bucket of ice water.

To escape, Gritter dodged—naked—out an open door and into the winter cold. Baumann slammed the door shut and laughed as Gritter bawled to be let back in. A few minutes later, we heard Gritter coming down the stairs from the front of the building, all the while hollering that he was going to get Baumann.

Finally, Gritter stepped into the shop, and Baumann collapsed with renewed laughter at the sight of him. At no point in Gritter's trek—from the back of the building, around to the front door, and then down the stairs to the shop—had he bothered to transfer his shorts from his hand to their rightful position.

This, I was shocked to learn, was no extraordinary scene inside the Missouri State Penitentiary in the 1980s.

A lot has changed in Missouri Corrections in the thirty years since then. Now, the only scenes inside the Missouri State

---

* Names and identifying information of all prisoners and some staff have been changed.

Penitentiary are of tourism. The old institution closed on September 15, 2004, when operations moved to the new Jefferson City Correctional Center across town. Much of the Missouri State Penitentiary, or MSP, has been torn down, and what remains is a sort of museum. Visitors come to get up close to a violent history.

Promotional materials for MSP tours promise stories of infamous prisoners—such as Sonny Liston, "Pretty Boy" Floyd, and James Earl Ray, to name a few of the favorites—as well as tales of riots, escapes, executions, and even the paranormal. Such draws work well on brochures, but once inside the walls, most visitors will begin wondering about daily life. They will view the cold, empty buildings and want to know, "What was it like to live and work in such a place?"

Few visitors can imagine scenes like the one of Gritter bouncing from the shower out into the winter cold to avoid a staff member's practical joke. Or of a rookie maintenance supervisor taking convicts bearing wrenches and saws into the gloom of an underground plumbing tunnel, home to roaches and rats. Or of prisoners lining up for a pancake restaurant that two entrepreneurial cellmates launched from their shared cell. But these are the scenes I recall from MSP.

I began working at MSP on February 21, 1984, and was there through the institution's close. I began at the bottom rung in maintenance and finished my career in February 2010 as the chief engineer at the new institution. While my later positions offered much more prestige, it was in my early years, when I worked directly with the inmates, that I made my favorite memories. Long before MSP shut down, I started writing down some of my experiences to share in the MSP personnel club's monthly newsletter, *State Pen*. Several of my coworkers expressed interest in seeing the stories put into a book, so after I retired, with the help of my daughter Anita Neal Harrison, a professional writer and editor, I did just that.

Rather than writing one long narrative, we have chosen to

Larry Neal renovating the old canteen into the new
captain's shack in the late 1980s.

make this book a collection of stories. One point to note is that
in these stories, I do not attempt to answer what life was like
behind the MSP walls from all perspectives or at all times. These
stories are all told from the perspective I had in the early part
of my career as a maintenance worker, with most of the events
taking place between 1984 and 1996. Because I was a "square
man"—convict slang for a staff member who is not an officer—

Historic photo of what was then and is now again the front entrance of the Missouri State Penitentiary. The building is Housing Unit 1, built in 1905. Photo from the collection of Mark Schreiber.

the inmates did not consider me an enemy but someone who was there to make their lives better. I got to be friends, or at least friendly, with many of the workers assigned to my crews. These relationships afforded me a close view of what life was like for them locked up in MSP, and I've shared that view in these stories.

Working in maintenance also afforded me an intimate view of the old institution itself: the housing units, service buildings, tunnels, towers, and walls that were MSP. The State of Missouri opened the MSP at the very time the Alamo was under siege in Texas in 1836, a quarter century *before* the Civil War, and the facility was one hundred years old by the time the prison at Alcatraz opened. Its past was never farther than a shovel scoop away. I found the history fascinating and wrote several descriptions of its buildings when MSP was still in use.

A few of my coworkers whose histories at MSP didn't extend so far back as mine doubted the truthfulness of some of my tales published in *State Pen*. Others reminded me of things I should write about. Some of the maintenance staff complained from the beginning that I ran down the Engineering Department, which was in charge of all of maintenance. One officer said to me, "If even half of those stories are true, you're telling on yourself an awful lot."

He was right. I only confessed to things I did to explain how it was back then, rather than in defense for doing them. I'm sure it sounds odd to some, but in the twenty years I worked at MSP, I came to love and admire the old institution, and having witnessed major changes in its operations, I realized no one would be able to guess what life used to be like inside MSP. Some of it was hilarious, some was tragic, and some of it was just mind-boggling. But life inside MSP was always interesting.

Chapter 1

Learning from the Master

"No Legs." That's what we called him. He really wasn't a bad sort of guy, except he loved to aggravate the living daylights out of anybody who got within ten feet of him. I don't think he would have intentionally given anyone a permanent injury, but short of that, there wasn't a whole lot he wouldn't do. His name was Ed Hanauer, and when I first met him, I thought people were awfully mean to him. Then I found out that being mean to Hanauer was a survival skill that people acquired upon spending just a little time with him.

Hanauer was the lead supervisor in the MSP plumbing shop when I was assigned to it in 1984. This assignment came seven months into my MSP career, and when I arrived at the plumbing shop I was amazed at how much horsing around went on in the whole maintenance building. Dubbed M&M, this building housed the labor, refrigeration, paint, carpenter, and electric shops on the main level, and the machine and plumbing shops in the basement. Pranks, tormenting, and a warped sense of humor permeated the whole place. While the antics made me uneasy at first, I soon came to see the free-for-all atmosphere as a good thing. It offered relief from the constant tension that the inmates endured elsewhere in the pen. It was a place for kidding around, and the convicts and staff both seemed to appreciate it.

Most of the pranks in the plumbing shop got their start with Hanauer, who was nicknamed No Legs because his legs were extremely short in proportion to the rest of him. Hanauer had been working at the pen since the 1970s and was perfectly at ease with

Ed "No Legs" Hanauer, Larry Neal, and Richard Baumann at Hanauer's desk in the plumbing shop in the early 1990s.

the inmates. Some of his favorite tricks were clamping an inmate's foot in a vise, tying their shoelaces in knots, or turning the fire hose on them when they were in the shower. The inmates were constantly trying to get even, but Hanauer would always manage to turn the tables on them. One time after the inmates had jammed his desk drawers shut, he put two wax rings in the plumbing shop clothes dryer. For the next two weeks, every time the inmates tried to put their clothes on, they would slide back off.

One of Hanauer's favorite targets was Gritter, a good ol' boy from Arkansas. Gritter and I got along pretty good because we were both raised so far out in the country that we considered a town with a population over one hundred to be a pretty big place. I was raised in the backwoods of Brumley, Missouri, population eighty-seven, in a three-room farmhouse that wouldn't be considered fit for human habitation now. The "bathroom" was about one hundred feet from the back door, and the next neighbors, who lived about a mile up Glaize Creek, thought of us as high-tone and uppity because we had electricity in the house. Gritter and I were country, we were hillbilly, and we weren't ashamed of it (still hain't). But we did get a lot of grief over it.

Whenever Hanauer would walk into the shop, his first order of business was to jab the nearest inmate in the ribs to see how high he would jump. When he found one who was goosey, he would always look for an opportunity to attack. Gritter, Hanauer found, was just such a mark. Despite his mass, Gritter had a high-pitched voice that sounded all kinds of wrong combined with his hillbilly drawl. It was a joy to see him jump and hear him squeak, and Hanauer was determined to get all the enjoyment he could get.

Also making Gritter a favorite target was the fact that for a big fella and a country boy, he was awfully afraid of rats, snakes, and some of the bigger bugs. I always liked taking Gritter into one of the underground MSP tunnels because all I had to do to get him going was to stop suddenly, shine my flashlight under some pipes, and ask, "What's that?" Then as Gritter wildly looked around, I could just barely touch down low on his leg with the end of a pipe wrench. That never failed to get a great reaction. If Hanauer had been with us, I know he would've been proud.

The underground tunnels were eerie places. Steam pipes, water pipes, electrical conduit, telephone wires, and patched sewer pipes ran through these arteries of the institution. Escaping steam filled the tunnels with a haze of fog, and there was little overhead light. When I first started working in maintenance, the tunnels were lit with incandescent bulbs that hung from wires. The bulbs were spaced about every fifty feet, but only a few of them worked some of the time. (Eventually, we installed por-celain fixtures about every twenty feet, and most of the bulbs worked most of the time.)

The tunnels had arched, brick-lined ceilings, most about five feet high (leaving plenty of head room for Hanauer). A lot of the bricks were missing, with mold and slime growing on the walls. Most of the fiberglass insulation that was supposed to cover the steam pipes had fallen in ragged chunks to the floor. Fiberglass insulation causes a painful itch on people, but the MSP rats, which numbered in the thousands, seemed to find it a most comfortable nesting material. The rats also appreciated the tunnels' warmth; thanks to the steam pipes, the temperature might be 130 degrees up where the humans

Inside one of the underground tunnels a few weeks after MSP closed. The big pipes on the left are for steam and return condensate, and the smaller pipes on the right are for hot water and electrical conduit.

had to breathe, but it was much cooler down on the floor where the rats lived.

Navigating through the tunnels required strict attention, as some of our primitive maintenance predecessors had run pipes or supports from one side to the other in the most unlikely places. These unexpected additions tended to be at about eye level, which put them in the perfect position for whacking the heads of intruders who were not looking straight ahead but down at the floor, or

```
TO:     Louis Markway, Supervisor M&M Building

FROM:   Larry Neal, Maintenance Supervisor I

SUBJECT:  CONDITIONS OF TUNNELS IN H.HALL (Housing Unit I)


     On this date, February 2, 1987, the Plumbing Shop received a
call to work on sink water to cell #6 of H.U. 1. We had to go into
the tunnel to make the necessary repairs.

     Because of the trash and junk it is almost impossible to get
into tunnel at all and extremely difficult to work on anything.
Junk covers the walk and is stacked against both walls until the
Plumbing pipes are covered. One of my Inmates, ███████████ #███
███ got tangled in an old fan cover and fell tearing his pants and
scratching his leg; And, could have very easily been badly injured.
Any inspection made by a safty inspector could possibly have result-
ed in my being cited for negligence for even taking an Inmate into
this area.

     There are pieces of old metal cell tables; legs, part of fans,
broken chairs, parts of old washing machine's, broken light bulbs,
case's of gallon disinfectant-so old the box's have rotted, box's
of books, parts of old metal beds and all kinds of paper trash in
this tunnel.

     Also, the conditions of the metal walls between tunnel and cells
is in an extremely deteriated state. This condition is so far advanced
that areas large enough to put your head through are rusted completely
away, and it is possible that an area large enough for an inmate to
crawl through could possibly be kicked or knocked into these walls.

     If Inmate's with the destructive abilities and intentions such as
we have had dealings with that are housed in H.U. 2 were housed in these
cells-it is my personal belief they could keep M&M busy with repairs
everyday of the week.

     It isn't my intention to place blame on anyone; nor, do I know what
procedures are possible for the correction of these problems(except for
the removal of the trash and the junk), but I do feel it is my obligation
as an employee to bring this to your attention.
```

An interoffice communication of February 1987 from Neal to his supervisor about unsafe conditions inside Housing Unit 1 plumbing tunnels.
These plumbing tunnels were inside the building.

at what might be *on* the floor. It took me more times than I like to
admit to realize that when someone suddenly cursed and said, "Ow!"
ahead of me, I should duck (but not too low because the problem
might not be a pipe but a rat coming towards us, and it's somewhat
unsettling to meet one eyeball to eyeball). There were also old support remnants that stuck out a few inches from the walls.

All of these hazards combined to create a daunting obstacle course. If I were looking down, I could bounce my poor head off a brace and slump against a wall, where one of the support remnants might stab me in the arm, then the tunnel slime would slip me down onto the fiberglass-covered floor, and a bloodthirsty rat might be staring me in the face, wondering if perhaps I was there for supper.

Once, after I had been with Hanauer long enough to pick up some of his habits, I took Gritter on an errand in Tunnel 3, which was one of the oldest and creepiest in the pen. Suddenly, I came to a stop and shone my flashlight under the tunnel's steam pipe.

"Whoa! Gritter, look at that rat over there!" I exclaimed.

Gritter tried to hide his anxiety. "Neal, don't do that," he ordered. "Don't play around like that."

"I'm serious, Gritter. Can't you see him?"

Peering where I had pointed, Gritter's high voice became more strained. "Quit it, Neal!"

"No! Look! There's two of 'em! Big ones!"

Beginning to back up, Gritter snapped, "Neal, quit kidding around. That ain't funny."

"I'm not kidding! Look, one of them is wearing sunglasses! See them?"

"You'd better quit!" He was still backing away. "I'm scared of them things. That ain't funny!"

"And that one's got a patch over his eye! See them?"

"Neal," Gritter said, "I'm gonna have to kill you."

Another time, I took Gritter and a capable inmate named Jimmy to a tunnel under the staff dining room. The tunnel was only about three feet high and three feet wide, so we had to crawl through it. It went about five feet, then turned, went about twenty feet and then turned again. I sent Gritter and Jimmy in to fix a small leak that was just past the second bend. Because we only

had one flashlight, I waited at the tunnel door, confident there
was nowhere for them to go but back to where I waited for them.

I continued waiting until I thought enough time had passed
for them to have fixed the leak twice and then I decided I would
have to go in and check on my charges. I had to go slow, as I had
no light and I had to straddle an uninsulated four-inch steam
pipe. As I made my way, about every fifteen seconds I could
hear Gritter mumble something I couldn't understand, and then
Jimmy would say, "Hold the light down here where I can see."
When I turned the last corner, without being observed, I stopped
and watched them. Gritter, bent over and on his knees, would
hold the light on the pipe that Jimmy was working on for a few
seconds and would then shine the light on the ceiling, which
was only inches above his head and back. In a voice that actually
quivered, Gritter would whimper, "Look at the size of those cockroaches." Then Jimmy would patiently but firmly say, "Hold the
light down here where I can see."

I hadn't noticed until then, but the ceiling was covered with
enormous roaches, about the size of my little finger. I guess the
vermin hid out down there until the dining room was empty and
dark and it was time to get supper. When Gritter would shine
the light on these creepy-crawlies, it seemed the whole tunnel
ceiling would move and swirl. As quietly as I could, I picked up a
handful of gravel off the floor, and when he shone the light down
on the pipe again, I tossed the gravel on Gritter's back.

Unfortunately, his first reaction was to try to jump up, and
the sudden halt to his progress caused him to drop the light. This
plunged the tunnel into total darkness, so I lost video and had
to settle for audio. Simultaneous to the lights going off came a
choked-off scream. Then I heard a lot of bumping, thumping, and
grunting. It sounded like Gritter had decided to stand up, and
it sounded like maybe he had made it. Next, it sounded like he
was running but not going anywhere. His breath was coming in
ragged gasps, and then came this long, drawn-out, low whimper-

ing moan. About that time, Jimmy got the light back on, saw me, said, "Hi, Neal," and went back to work.

Gritter was on his hands and knees, with his head against a tunnel wall, crawling in place for all he was worth. He stopped, turned his head sideways, and looked at me. All of that happened in a matter of seconds. When he turned towards me, the light was behind him, but I could tell that the look he gave me did not bode well for my health. I knew how to divert his attention though. I looked at him with concern and said, "Man, did you see that rat run down through here? I guess I scared it because it took off running towards you guys and just before the light went out, it looked like it jumped up on your back." Gritter rose to a squat and turned a quick circle, which was quite a feat in itself, considering Gritter's size, the number of pipes he had to negotiate, and the limited space available. Then he kind of slumped against the wall, looked at me a moment, and spit a stream of tobacco juice on a steam pipe. He watched it until the sizzling stopped, and then in a sad defeated voice he said, "Neal, don't *do* that to me." He brushed some cockroaches off his shirt, shuddering as he did so, and still panting for breath, added, "Man, you sure had me going there for a minute."

When we got back to the shop I, of course, boasted about my triumph. Hanauer took me aside and told me I needed to treat my inmate workers better, that I couldn't be causing them to have conniption fits in tunnels. "At least," he added, confidentially, "not unless I'm there to see it."

Chapter 2

Into the Lions' Den

As much fun as I had at MSP, it's ironic how much I initially dreaded going to work there. I think before sharing any more experiences, I should back up and relate just what it was like getting used to the place.

The truth is, I had no desire to go to work in a maximum-security prison. The first time an old metal door banged shut and trapped me inside, I had a sudden onset of claustrophobia. It happened right as I came through the front entrance. To get into the prison, one had to go through two sets of staff-operated sliding doors. The first had opened, I had stepped inside, and then the door slammed shut behind me, locking me in a holding space. I looked at the officer in the bubble, and if he could've heard me, I would've told him, "If you will open that door back up and let me out of here, I'll leave and never bother you all again."

It was a good thing I couldn't talk to him because my wife would've been awfully upset if I'd quit before I'd even gotten started. It had been her idea that I leave a steady construction job to go to work for the state so our family, which included daughters aged eleven, eight, and two, would have health insurance. I'd never been too concerned about having insurance, but I could see how a job at a maximum-security penitentiary would need good medical benefits.

In the beginning, each day brought some new unnerving experience. My first impressions were made during a week of training. Looking back, I believe the real purpose of MSP training wasn't to educate the new hires but to weed out the squeamish

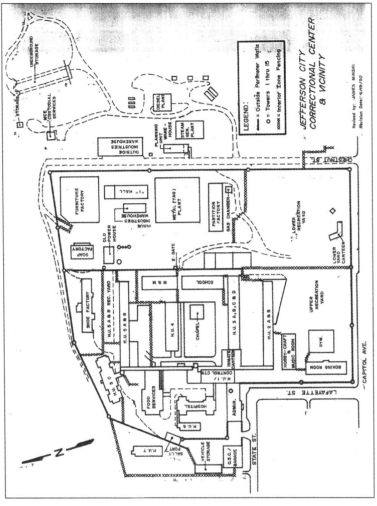

This diagram of MSP (from when it was called the Jefferson City Correctional Center) was given to new employees during training. MSP was renamed the Jefferson City Correctional Center in 1991 and the name reverted to MSP during construction of the new facility.

and fearful. Little was said about how to handle situations, while most of the time was spent on old blood-and-guts war stories.

Part of our training was to spend some time following a "corrections officer," the then-new term for a guard. I was assigned to one in Housing Unit 3-A. As we made the rounds through the cell house, he shared stories about all the fights he had been in and the convicts he'd seen cut up. He told me every convict had a homemade weapon—a shank—and just ached for a chance to use it. I believed him. Then it was noon, and he went down the walk yelling, "Main line!" (meal time) and unlocked cell door after cell door with a big key on a ring full of big keys. He never looked back to see whether anyone was exiting the cells he was unlocking.

I felt the hair on the back of my neck rising. I didn't know why the officer had a death wish and I certainly didn't understand why he hadn't let me hide before carrying out his convict-assisted suicide. Seeing no better option, I kept walking behind him and was more amazed with each step that we had gotten as far as we had without attack. We circled around at the far end of the building and came up the other side of the cellblock, where he continued to unlock cells. Then we made the complete circle again so he could relock what he had just opened. After that we went up to three and four walks, the next two levels, and did the same until we had unlocked and relocked every cell in 3-A. Then the officer escorted me out of the building, and I felt a renewed thankfulness that I served the same God who had delivered Daniel from the lions' den.

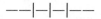

Another memorable event from training was the tour of the institution all of us new hires took together. Before working at the pen, I had imagined that the inmates spent almost all of their time locked up in their cells. I discovered, with some distress, that this was not the case. In some of the housing units, the prisoners were locked up in their cells only at night or under special circumstances, while a few areas of the pen, such as the ice plant and the laundry, even had quarters for the couple of inmates who worked there. Hundreds of inmates throughout the pen got out of their housing units to work with assigned supervisors (like I was to be), while others were porters, or janitors, who moved about under just the general supervision of officers.

I believed I was about to witness a fatal flaw in this approach as our little tour group entered Housing Unit 5-C, also known as Supermax, the housing unit for the most difficult inmates. Our training officer, Allen Sartain, was walking right along, not the least bit concerned about bringing us all so close to these dangerous criminals, when Mr. Clean stepped out in front of him.

It wasn't really Mr. Clean, of course. This dude looked a whole lot meaner. He was naked to the waist and seemed to be nothing but powerful cords of muscle wrapped on top of other muscle. His waist was narrow and his shoulders and arms were massive. He had a shaved head and wore an earring chained to a nose ring. He didn't live in 5-C—the 5-C inmates were restricted to their cells—but worked there as a porter.

He had stepped out so suddenly that Sartain halted with his face just inches from the inmate's bare chest. The whole class took a quick step backwards and with bated breath waited to see what was going to happen next. I wondered if we had a backup instructor, or how one would be found, and what would be done with us in the meantime. The inmate, with a sneer on his lip, said something about Sartain filling our heads with a bunch of lies and then reached down and began to straighten the officer's tie. To my amazement and admiration, Sartain neither backed up nor even flinched, but began talking to this fearsome character like an old friend. Sartain then told him to get out of his way because he had a job to do. With a big smile, the inmate stepped aside, but when Sartain's back was to us, the inmate dropped his smile and glared at each of us as we filed past.

It was also in training that I was first introduced to the

The light-colored stone building is Housing Unit 1, now the front entrance to MSP. To the right is the administration building, and to the left
is the hospital. Both of these buildings were torn after the MSP closed.

warped logic behind so many of the pen's rules and regulations.
During one of the training officer's lectures, he informed us that
we would not be allowed to carry pocketknives. I raised my hand.

"I'll be working in maintenance, so that rule won't apply to
me, right?"

The officer shook his head.

"No, maintenance workers are no exception," he said,
adding, "You've got to realize, you will be working with inmates.
What would happen if they stole your pocketknife and threatened you with it?"

It made sense at the time. Then I went to work.

As a labor supervisor, I was in charge of a crew of inmates.
These inmates could go to the tool room and borrow every kind
of tool imaginable. For the work we did on the labor crew, picks
and shovels were the tools most often needed. My job was to lead

these tool-bearing convicts to wherever there was a maintenance problem requiring laborers. This might mean taking them to I-Hall to use their picks to break up salt stored there for use in the powerhouse, but it could also involve leading them to some secluded back corner to dig up a busted pipe.

The good news was I had protective gear. I remember how relieved all of us new recruits were when we got to that part of training. Back then, square men did not receive radios, Mace, batons—nothing like that. But we got a whistle.

"Here is your protection," the training officer said, as he dangled a whistle. "If you blow your whistle, someone will come running to help."

Later, I discovered that whistles garnered much the same reaction as car alarms in parking lots.

When training ended and real work began, I still believed I would never feel at ease inside the prison. But I was determined to give it a go. I didn't have to wait long for the first test of my mettle. Much of my time as labor supervisor was to be spent supervising the delivery of tools, paint, and ice. The four to six inmate laborers on my crew loaded and unloaded the truck, an old short-bed Chevy. Bill Wieberg, the maintenance supervisor in charge of inside maintenance, told me that he wouldn't leave me on my own for the first few weeks. My first day Warren Johnson, the other labor supervisor, rode with my crew and me.

But my second day, Johnson wasn't there, and Wieberg asked if I remembered how to get to the ice plant by myself.

"I'm sure I do," I responded.

"I hate to send you out with the labor crew alone on your second day here, but I need the ice delivered, and everyone else is busy," he said. "Don't worry about getting lost. The inmate driver you have knows how to get there, and they know what to do when they get there." He seemed more concerned that I might be scared than that I might run into trouble, and I didn't want to make a bad impression.

"No problem," I said. "I'll round up my crew and head on over."

But I wasn't so confident. I didn't know my way around the pen, and it was easy to get turned around in the maze of buildings. It was with much relief that I parked the truck and walked into the ice plant. I turned down the dark corridor where the few inmates who worked in the plant had their living quarters and yelled at them to get up and get some ice out. Suddenly out of the darkness, a huge convict came running towards me. He was in his underwear and was screaming and crazed. My first thought was to turn and run. My second thought was that I couldn't show any fear. I stood my ground, and he skidded to a stop right in front of me. But he didn't slow in his ranting and raging. I was finally able to understand that he was upset with us for coming too early; he told me I wasn't supposed to show up there until such and such a time.

"Wieberg sent me for ice," I responded in a matter-of-fact tone. "You load it, and we'll leave you alone."

He glared at me a moment longer and then turned and disappeared into the darkness. He returned with his clothes all on and went into the ice plant where he began to drag out barrels. A few minutes later his partner came up to help.

After we got away and I reflected on how I had handled the situation, I felt a little more confident that perhaps I could make it working at the pen. If the convict had in fact had a club or a knife in his hand, then I would have lost a lot of confidence, and possibly my head, and I doubt then that my wife would've felt so good about encouraging me to work at the pen, no matter how well it paid my medical bills.

Chapter 3

A Word about Sewers

One thing I learned at MSP is that there are absolutely unlimited possibilities of things that can go wrong with prison sewer systems and to the courageous people who work on them.

Prior to working at the pen, I had been a construction worker with experience in concrete, carpentry, and installing plumbing. I had no experience with sewer maintenance. Well, that's not quite true. When I was still a kid, living on the farm, I had helped repair our "sewer system." Basically, we would dig a new hole and move the little building. I, being a little smarter than my little brother, carefully avoided the area where it had last been situated.

When I started at the pen as a labor supervisor, I did not have any direct dealings with maintaining the plumbing, except for the occasions when I was called on to help haul large tools or parts with the labor truck. One such time came about three months into my prison career when I got a call to take the big sewer auger machine out to Louie Markway. Markway was a second-tier maintenance supervisor and was assigned to take care of the MSP grounds and buildings located outside the perimeter walls. While most of the prison facilities were inside the walls, some—including a housing unit for convicts soon headed back to society—stood outside the stone perimeter.

Markway and George Frank, a first-tier maintenance supervisor, were trying to unstop a sewer that ran out under the wall in the area of the Special Management Facility, the behavior modification and administrative segregation unit that made MSP a

Department of Corrections and Human Resources
MISSOURI STATE PENITENTIARY FOR MEN
INTER-OFFICE COMMUNICATION

To: Mr. Rutledge, A.W.S.S. et.al.   Date: June 24, 1986

From: Mr. ░░░░░░░░░░░░░░░░░░░░ Larry Neal, Maintenance Supervisor I

Subject: Plumbing Problems of Housing Unit #2A & B

On June 23, 1986, I had to unstop main sewerline from H.U. 2A&B; also, others involved were, Mr. Markway, Maintenace Supervisor II and Mr. George Frank, Maintenance Supervisor I spent eight hours Saturday trying to unstop this manhole. We found about six bushel baskets of mostly empty bread sacks(the ones that are used in the main kitchen). In order to clean this out of the manholes it was necessary to shutoff all water to housing unit 2 and pump out the manholes.

Anytime water is shutoff and then turned back on in a housing unit, enough debris from the waterlines is loosened to cause many stools to go into a continuous flush. So, about 2:00pm when we finally got the manholes cleaned out we immediately went to H.U. 2 and went into each tunnel and checked each stool in the housing unit to see that they would shutoff.

During this time, the inmates on 5&6 walks on B side had stopped up their sewers and we unstopped them while we were there. We also took care of 2 or 3 other problems while we were there that the officers had brought to our attention. At approximately 4:00pm when we had all serious problems taken care of and the Sgt was asking if we had time to unstop a few sinks I told him we would come back in the morning but I needed to get my inmate plumber to mainline for chow(it was hot the 24 hour plumber). The Sgt agreed that was alright with him. Soon after we had left, they called the 24 hour plumber, Inmate ░░░░░░ # ░░░░ and he then also checked the hall and found no serious problems. The following morning we returned(Tues 24, June,1986) and made these repairs: unstopped sink in cells 318, 180 and 66; put a new hosebib faucet in cell 134 and put a handle repairkit on cell 120 and a vacuuum breaker on cell 153 and had no other problems reported to us that were called to the M&M shop or sent in a workorder. None of theses problems would keep a man from using his stool or getting a drink. It did mean a man might have to dip out his sink or temporaoly put up with some dripping leak for one night. The point being- all of the above problems could have been avoided by someone stopping the certain Inmate's that had carried the 6 baskets of plastic sacks into their cells and flushing them down their stools (Drains).

cc: Mr. Elmer Larkins, Chief Engineer MSP
     Mr. Larry Neal, Maintenance Supervisor I M&M
     M&M Office Files.

RECEIVED
JUN 26 1986
ASSOCIATE WARDEN
SUPPORT SERVICES

A June 1986 interoffice communication from Neal alerting Associate Warden Leonard Rutledge to problems with the sewer system.

super-maximum prison. SMF was a prison inside the prison and consisted of three halls, 5-A, 5-B, and 5-C, each with its own level of restriction. The most restrictive was Housing Unit 5-C, also known as Supermax. This was the housing unit that was used to lock down the really bad boys, those inmates who were in constant trouble for making hooch, fighting, making and selling shanks, harassing the staff, attempting escape, and other such shenanigans.

I helped to carry the auger machine up to the area where it was needed. Having never witnessed this odd drilling contraption in action, I waited to see how it worked. We were in an isolated area on the back side of the prison, next to the train tracks by the Missouri River. No inmates were involved, it was a nice warm spring day, and I thought I would relax and enjoy the morning.

As I watched Frank and Markway set up the auger, I innocently wondered aloud what could stop up a twelve-inch sewer pipe.

"Probably a mattress," Frank commented.

I blinked. "You couldn't get a mattress in the sewer," I said.

"Can if you tear it up in small enough pieces," he answered, as he began to run the auger into the sewer pipe.

"Why would you do that?" I asked.

"*I* wouldn't," he answered without looking up.

"Why would *they* do that?" I responded.

"'Cause they're inmates," he said, and he finally looked at me. "Inmates want to stop up the sewers."

Frank and Markway then explained that inmates would tear up their sheets, blankets, towels, clothes, pillows, and whatever else they could get their hands on and flush the scraps just to create problems. It was an especially favored pastime in Supermax, where the inmates were locked down for as long as six months without television sets, radios, books (except law or religious material), or even cigarettes. In that environment, someone coming in to unstop their toilet was a diversion to anticipate, and it wasn't as if they were wasting their time because they weren't going to be doing anything with their time anyway. I found, in talking to inmates later, that many of them felt it was their duty to destroy as much state property as possible. As they explained it to me, the more it cost the state to keep them locked up, the quicker the Department

of Corrections would run out of money and the more criminals
would have to be turned loose to balance the books.

This worked especially well with things the public expected
prisoners to have access to, such as law books. Many times,
inmates researching their cases would simply tear out the pages
that pertained to them, and then other inmates trying to use
books with missing pages would file lawsuits because the state
wasn't furnishing them with the necessary resources to fight
their convictions in court. These inmates were well aware of their
constitutional right to sue the state for wrongfully incarcerating
them for crimes they had committed but would never have been
convicted for had the courts protected their rights.

But I digress. In order to unstop a sewer, you must first get
access to the inside of the pipe. This is normally achieved inside a
manhole, where the open ends of pipes offer a place to insert the
auger. In this case, normal wasn't the chosen option. Using the kind
of ingenuity that I found to be common in Corrections workers,
someone had used a saw to cut a hole about three inches wide by
ten inches long in the top of the large pipe where it was exposed
coming out from the wall, and into this hole Frank was running the
auger. When he would hook onto something, he'd pull the auger
back out, and in this way, he pulled out about three bedsheets and a
shoe, and then he hooked into something solid. We all three pulled
and tugged, grunted and sweated, and finally fell over backwards
when the auger came loose from whatever we had hooked.

At this point I asked if it might not be simpler to go inside
the walls, open a manhole on the other side of the obstruction,
and pull from the direction the obstruction had gone in instead of
pulling it on through the pipe. They laughed and explained that the
blockage had caused the manhole to overflow with sewage water
until it was buried under some three feet of water (the officer in the
tower said it looked like a small lake), and even if we could get to
the pipe and hook the obstruction, we could never pull it against
that kind of pressure.

We worked at it for about another half an hour and piled up quite an assortment of inmate clothing and bedding. Then Frank yelled, "Here it comes!" I bent over to see, if I could, what we had been pulling on for so long as it went by in the pipe. Nobody had explained to me how the forces of nature would react when a ton of water (and a ton of various other things) rushing through a twelve-inch pipe intercepted a thirty-square-inch hole in the top of said pipe, nor how the laws of dynamics would allow a large quantity of water (along with all of the aforementioned other things) to suddenly change directions and burst forth out of the top of the pipe as a mighty geyser.

Now, had I taken the time to sit and contemplate the subject, I might have figured it all out by myself. Or if I had observed the hasty retreat of Markway and Frank—two cowards who, thinking only of saving themselves, had abandoned me to my sad fate—then I might at least have turned my head. If I had even remembered the old adage, "Curiosity killed the cat," I might not have bent over to look. Sadly, I must tell you that none of these happened. What did happen when that horrid nasty brew burst out of the pipe is almost too awful to relate. I quickly stepped back and turned my head up to escape the awful torrent erupting in my face. Unfortunately, as I threw my head back, I hadn't time to realize that what goes up must come down. And down it came. Now I was saturated head to foot with water and other unmentionable stuff. Finally, I stepped into the clear, and certain that I had somehow been set up, I looked at Frank and Markway.

They were both staring at me, eyes wide, mouths gaping, with a look of astonishment and horror on their faces. You would think it would take at least a little while for a person's emotions to go from horrific astonishment to uncontrollable mirth. Nope. In mid-blink, Frank and Markway went from shock to tears-rolling, side-splitting, donkey-braying laughter. I stood there with dripping wet chunks falling off me, and it was laugh or cry. I decided to join the crowd and laugh, but I don't think I enjoyed it nearly as much as they did.

Finally, Markway decided to try to help me out. First, he took me up to State Surplus Property to find me some clothes to change into. To my dismay, he also felt obligated to share what he seemed to think was the funniest thing he had ever seen with every person we ran into. When people would begin to realize what I was wet with, they would invariably begin to shift uncomfortably and back away. They would take little steps, as if trying not to offend me or hoping I wouldn't notice, but still increasing the distance between us.

Markway took me out to Housing Unit 7, the housing unit outside the walls, so I could shower and change. I started at the top, lathering my head up with a bar of soap, when I suddenly realized I was in a penitentiary shower, alone, and with so much soap on my head and in my eyes and ears that I couldn't see or hear anyone, even if they were right behind me. I washed it off as quickly as I could, saw to my relief that I was still alone, and finished my shower. Then I put on the clothes that Markway had gotten for me—old inmate clothes complete with numbers. Later I learned from Frank that Markway had chosen those clothes because he thought it would be funny to have me dressed up like an inmate; there had been a lot of army green and camouflage available. The rest of the day was pretty much uneventful except anytime I sat down, anyone close found an excuse to get up and move.

Now I know a lot more about sewer systems, and in retrospect I have to wonder if I really was any smarter than my little brother.

Chapter 4

Life in the Pen

I reckon that people who haven't worked in a prison would have a hard time picturing—or believing—what the atmosphere was like in the Missouri State Penitentiary during the 1980s.

One of the things that took some getting used to was the talk. I'd never heard the kind of language that was used in the pen—and I was a Navy veteran. Nine-tenths of every sentence was vulgarity of the filthiest kind, and it took at least ten words to say "yes" or "no." The most common phrase worked into almost every sentence two (or even three) times had to do with incest with a female parent. I know I am occasionally given to exaggeration, but in this case, that would not be possible. That particular phrase had become a habit with almost all of the inmates and most of the staff and was inserted into speech without the speakers even realizing it.

Even what would have been considered pretty rough language on the street would have been mild inside the walls. I was taken aside and warned by one of the officers that I wasn't going to last very long if I didn't learn to talk like an inmate. He said that if I wanted them to take me seriously, I should curse them out in their own language. He told me that he didn't like to use those kinds of words either, but if he didn't, he couldn't get any respect from them. I found out I did all right without it; in fact, many of the convicts respected me for not stooping to that level.

The vulgarities weren't all that set communication apart inside the pen. There was also the prison slang. For example, I learned "burning bread" on someone meant wishing or mention-

ing something bad that might come to pass, "hanging a writ" was
to file a lawsuit, and "get off in a wreak" meant to get in trouble.
Other vocabulary I picked up was "stinger," a homemade water
heater; "cadillac," a weighted string used to move things from one
cell to another; "checking in," when an inmate asked the administration to place him in protective custody; "get a ticket" or "get
paper put on you" or "get wrote up," have a written violation;
"get locked up" or "thrown in the hole," get placed in administrative segregation; "tips," the inmates' allowances or wages that
they used at the canteen; "posting the tips," when the inmates'
tips went on their accounts (a monthly occurrence); "green
money," real U.S. currency; "a mule," a staff member who brings
things in to the inmates, usually by coercion; "turned," changed
into something you wouldn't have chosen to become, such as a
"mule"; "baking a cake," having homosexual relations that might
be vanilla or chocolate or either one with the other for icing;
"hooch" and "taterwater," homebrew; and "shank," a homemade
knife. Inmates were known to each other fondly as "celley,"
"homie," "homeboy," or "dog," along with the standard s.o.b. and
other such names, or despised as a "snitch," "punk," "woman,"
"homo," or "the warden's/captain's/lieutenant's/sergeant's boy,"
along with s.o.b as well.

On almost every wall of almost every building was posted
pornography. Nude photos spanned the range from mild to the
most graphic and obscene. Most cells had some photos up and
some had every square inch covered, including the ceiling and
the bottom of the top bunk. One of the more industrious inmates
had even wallpapered his combination sink/toilet with porn. Half
of the staff offices down inside the walls had some up, and if they
had an inmate clerk, there was more. This included maintenance,
factories, clothing issue, housing unit sergeants, power plant, ID,
and any other place where it wasn't expected that women would
be allowed to go and some places where it was. Later, such porn
was not allowed.

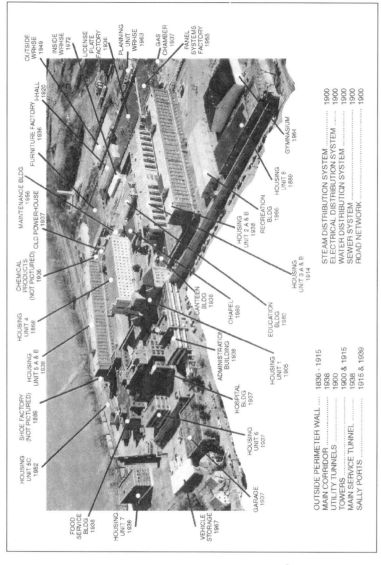

OUTSIDE WRHSE 1949
INSIDE WRHSE 1972
LICENSE PLATE FACTORY 1936
PLANNING UNIT WRHSE 1963
GAS CHAMBER 1937
PANEL SYSTEMS FACTORY 1955

FURNITURE FACTORY 1936
I-HALL 1920

MAINTENANCE BLDG 1956
OLD POWERHOUSE 1937
GYMNASIUM 1964
HOUSING UNIT 8 1889
RECREATION BLDG 1966
HOUSING UNIT 2 A & B 1938

CHEMICAL PRODUCTS (NOT PICTURED) 1936
HOUSING UNIT 3 A & B 1914

HOUSING UNIT 4 1868
HOUSING UNIT 5 A & B 1938
CANTEEN BLDG 1938
CHAPEL 1980
EDUCATION BLDG 1980

SHOE FACTORY (NOT PICTURED) 1889
ADMINISTRATION BUILDING 1938
HOUSING UNIT 1 1905

HOUSING UNIT 5C 1982
HOUSING UNIT 6 1937
HOSPITAL BLDG 1937

FOOD SERVICE BLDG 1938
HOUSING UNIT 7 1936
GARAGE 1937
VEHICLE STORAGE 1967

OUTSIDE PERIMETER WALL	1836 - 1915
MAIN CORRIDOR	1938
UTILITY TUNNELS	1900
TOWERS	1900 & 1915
MAIN SERVICE TUNNEL	1938
SALLY PORTS	1915 & 1939

STEAM DISTRIBUTION SYSTEM	1900
ELECTRICAL DISTRIBUTION SYSTEM	1900
WATER DISTRIBUTION SYSTEM	1900
SEWER SYSTEM	1900
ROAD NETWORK	1900

An aerial photo of MSP labeled with the names of buildings and their opening years. From the collection of Mark Schreiber.

There was a constant din inside the pen from inmates hollering and screaming. Windows were broken out of every housing unit and corridor, and the inmates were constantly shouting back and forth. Some of the hollering was good-natured and friendly, but most was insults and threats. It was especially loud in the mornings, when all of the inmates not in lockdown were let out of their cells at one time to go to breakfast and to work. There might be as many as seven or eight hundred men on the upper lawn at that time, and they would all be yelling back and forth. I was told that as long as they were noisy, it was okay; the time to be concerned was if the multitude got quiet—especially if the inmates were all in little groups sitting around watching, for that meant something big was about to go down. Most of the inmates knew where to get a shank in a hurry and would get one in a disturbance, if for no other reason than to protect themselves, but often with the idea of getting rid of an enemy if a good opportunity presented itself.

Gambling, drugs, and homosexual prostitution were controlled by those with enough power to enforce payment. Debts could grow quickly after a convict got involved in any of those activities because the amount of the debt usually doubled each time the due date came at the end of the month, when the wages and allowance funds inmates had coming were placed on their accounts. Often a smile and a cheery, "Don't worry about it, homie; you can catch me the next time they post the tips," was the response to an inmate unable to pay a small debt. That ploy would quickly accelerate the indebtedness beyond what could ever be paid. Then a young guy might be punked out, while others might be told to steal materials from their job, make a shank on the job (in a factory or in maintenance), or perform some other favor to pay on a debt that just kept growing. (Seems like when these convict bosses get out of prison, they could run credit card companies.) For those who refused, the choice became either try to stand up to the bosses' enforcers (and probably end up dead or badly injured) or check in to protective custody. Many of these bosses also had "stores" in their cells where they sold the items paid to them. The charge was two for one, payable when tips were posted and the inmate could go to the canteen.

Clothing was also used to pay debts. The state supplied inmates with gray shirts and pants, T-shirts, boxers, socks, and prison-made shoes. In the winter, inmates would get a set of insulated underwear (if their job took them outdoors) and a heavy waterproof coat. The insulated underwear was not given out until cold weather had permanently arrived, as on a warm day many inmates would trade them for nearly anything to other convicts who had a little more foresight. But prison issue could not hold a candle to the garments sent in from the outside.

I was shocked to learn that inmates wore street clothes inside the prison. Blue jeans were highly sought after, as were nicer shirts, good socks (the elastic in state socks left a lot to be desired), sweatshirts, jogging clothes, tennis shoes, dress shoes, and a list of other items too long to relate. The only way you could tell if someone was staff was if he was in uniform, and not everyone was. I could never tell the recreation officers from the inmates until I personally knew them. Inmates often had their "people" send in clothing just so they could erase a debt. Sometimes you could tell when a convict got in trouble with a debt because he'd suddenly be wearing state clothes and someone else would be wearing his cherished fashions.

Much of the state clothing would wind up in a trashcan or a sewer. One day, not long after I started, I watched an inmate come out of clothing issue with a new pair of work shoes that he was pulling the laces out of. He put the laces in his pocket, and the shoes in the first trash barrel he came to. I went into clothing issue and told the sergeant what I had just witnessed. He just shrugged his shoulders and said that the inmates got two pairs a year and could do whatever they wanted with them. In the spring, one of the signs that the convicts felt that warm weather was back to stay was trash barrels full of coats.

Many times before inmates went home, their last piece of business was to give their clothes, radio, television, and other belongings to their friends, either as a gift or for safekeeping until their eventual return. Seldom did inmates actually get their property returned to them, though, unless they were one bad son of a gun. Nowadays, personal belongings are tagged, marked, or engraved, and no inmate is allowed to have in his possession anything that once belonged to another inmate. But in the 1980s, clothes, shoes, televisions, radios, books, magazines, photographs of a nude or nearly nude wife, and any like item was a bartering tool used to pay debts, buy privileges, or spend on hooch and drugs.

When anyone convicted of a crime was sent to any of the prison camps in the state, their first stop was at MSP. Housing Unit 1 was receiving and diagnostic for the whole state. A busload of new inmates always created a lot of interest among the MSP inmates. Our maintenance inmates would use any excuse to get into Housing Unit 1 just to look around and see who was there. When these new inmates were sent down the corridor past the control center, it would be locked down and no one was allowed to cross. During these times, the convicts would crowd up to every window to watch those going by, yelling and jeering at the younger men, especially if their hair was a little long.

Some of this watching was to see if perhaps a known friend had come back, as was often the case, but much was watching for an enemy who might have to be dealt with. Also, in the eighties, the cell assignments were almost always done by inmate clerks. Many times I saw the convicts with money or power prowling the walks of Housing Unit 1 with a clerk. Several of my inmate workers told me that they would pay the clerks to assign the inmate of their choice to their cell. They would literally buy a cellmate. A scared young man assigned to the cell of a tough old convict had two choices: either fight and be beaten into submission every night until, perhaps, the old convict decided there was easier prey

Inmates returning to Housing Unit 2 after recreation in the Upper Yard of MSP in the 1980s. Photo from the collection of Mark Schreiber.

out there or become a punk and let the old convict own him. Homosexual activity was prevalent, and most of the guys I talked to estimated that anywhere from 50 to 80 percent of the population was engaged in some form of it, in spite of the fact that no one would admit their involvement.

There were numerous "girls" scattered throughout the camp—inmates who dressed and acted as if they were females and seemed to be accepted as such, not only by the inmates but also most of the staff. They were referred to as "she" and "her" or by their chosen female name. One that many talked about was said to be a former middleweight boxing champion who had started sex change hormones before being locked up and had gone to court to force the state to continue the treatment (he lost the case). He had pronounced breasts and claimed to be able to beat up any "John" who didn't pay up. Most of the inmate "girls" did not look very much like what they pretended to be and few would have been very convincing if they had been out of the prison setting. To many of the staff, these "girls" were a great source of amusement, and jokes about them, or other references, were commonplace. Although it was against the rules to allow them to wear makeup, few staff members wanted to get involved in enforcing that rule.

The inmates were offered a surprising amount of recreation, not just for their own sake but also for the management benefits it provided staff. Limiting recreation was a sanction that could be used to punish a conduct violation, but on the positive side, inmates who are tired from exercise are easier to handle than those who have no outlet for their energy except knocking heads together. Most of the recreation took place on the yards, and some of the favorite pastimes were basketball, handball, softball, and weightlifting, along with cards and dominoes. All of the recreation equipment was paid for with the profit from sales to inmates in the canteen.

Before I went to work at the pen, I imagined a place filled with hopelessness and despair, but most of the men locked up in that dreadful place seemed to have adapted and made the best of what life they had left. Inmates would laugh and joke, work, help each other, and engage in discussions on topics ranging from sports to religion. Some even appeared to have found what they had been looking for on the outside, and were content.

A lot went on in MSP, and what surprised me the most was that life went on there, too.

Chapter 5

You Call This an Emergency?

When I started as a labor supervisor, my days began at outside construction. Staff and inmates would load my truck up with supplies that had been ordered for inside. Much of it was for the housing units, mostly paint, rollers, and brushes. The rest was usually for the shops in M&M.

When I would finish with my deliveries, I would go sit in Bill Wieberg's office—he was the maintenance supervisor in charge of all of M&M—and I would wait until he had something else for me to do. An inmate clerk named Mark, who answered the phones for all of maintenance, was also there. When a housing unit would call with a problem, Mark would get on the intercom and call the needed shop. I was of the opinion that the plumbing shop was the laziest bunch of people in the institution, perhaps the world, as it would take them forever to respond to emergencies. The phone would ring and Mark would holler on the intercom, "Plumbing shop, you've got a flood in 3-House. A faucet broke off the wall in cell 126, and the water is spraying all over the place."

Silence.

"Plumbing shop, did you copy? You've got a flood in 3-A, 126."

"Yeah, we got it; we'll take care of it," would come the slow response.

Fifteen minutes or more would pass before the plumbing shop crew, led by Ed Hanauer and Richard Baumnn, would come dragging up the stairs. They'd be laughing and talking while some cell was getting wetter and wetter.

I was rather disgusted that Wieberg let them get away with such a pitiful attitude toward their work. I had no idea what I was in for when I moved into the plumbing shop, but Hanauer, generous soul that he is, was eager to bring me up, or in this case, down to speed.

I'd been in the shop about a month when I heard the first emergency call on the intercom: "Plumbing shop, you've got a busted faucet in death row, cell 46. It's spraying water all over the cell."

"All right," I answered. "We'll get it."

I then turned to the inmate workers. "Come on, guys, get some tools and a new hose bib, and let's go get that."

The inmates eyed me with disgust, Baumann and Hanauer smirked, and nobody moved.

"C'mon, guys," I repeated, with a twinge of impatience. "Let's fix this before it ruins all of the inmate's property."

Hanauer, with his feet on his desk and his chair tipped back against the wall, turned his attention from me to Baumann.

"Hose bib dripping?" Hanauer guessed.

"Probably needs a washer, unless the idiot just didn't get it all the way off," Baumann responded.

"They said it was spraying water all over," I reminded them.

Hanauer again turned to me and, with the air of one explaining the theory of molecular structure to a preschooler, said, "When they use the word *spraying*, that's a slow drip. *Flooding* means a faster drip to a steady run."

"Yeah, they're all a bunch of liars," Baumann said, taking in not just the inmates but staff too, "and no matter what it is that needs fixed, they are going to lie about it."

"Well," I said, "we still ought to get on over there and fix it. You never know. It might be serious."

Rivers, one of the plumbing shop inmates, spoke up. "Boy, Hanauer, they sure sent you a winner here. He just come off the banana boat?"

A death row cell in 1987. The "bricks" were drawn onto the wall by a bored prisoner. Photo from the collection of Mark Schreiber.

Then Rivers turned to me. "Didn't you hear them? They're just lying to you to get you to come over quicker. You don't want to encourage them."

I didn't argue anymore. I told them I was going to use the bathroom upstairs while they got ready to go. While I was up there, I called the officer who had called in the emergency, and he assured me that indeed water was going everywhere, and that if we didn't get there pretty quick, they would have to move the inmate to a different cell.

"It really is bad," he told me. "It's running out of his cell and into the cells around him."

When I got back downstairs, the others were ready to go. They ribbed me all the way over about the flood we were going to encounter when we got there. Inside I was laughing because I knew that there really was a flood. Because it was death row, the inmate had to be cuffed and removed from the cell. As I watched, I was a little surprised that I couldn't see any water coming out

on the floor. When we got into the cell all we found was a dripping faucet. When I asked the officer why he told me it was a
flood when it was only a drip, he said he was just going by what
the inmate walk man—an inmate hired to help clean a walk,
run errands, and communicate issues to the officers—had told
him, and no, he wasn't going to reprimand the inmate for lying
because it did need to be fixed and he did get us there.

The ribbing I took on the way back to the shop was even
worse than I had expected.

After that, I didn't get in quite so much of a hurry as I
learned the code: "broken steam lines" were drips, "no heat in a
housing unit" meant that at least one inmate complained of the
cold, and "a toilet that won't quit running" meant it doesn't shut
off as quickly as the inmate would like. I also found out that in a
real emergency, the officers would go in the housing unit's plumbing tunnel and turn off the water. It never failed to amaze me the
whoppers the officers would tell us to get us to come right away.
I don't know if they took the inmates' word or if they believed
exaggerating was the only way to get maintenance to come look
at a problem. And I worked at MSP for two years before I found
out that there was a work request system.

One day, several months into my time in the plumbing shop,
Hanauer responded to an "emergency" in the main dining room.
By this time, I thought I had heard every story inmates and staff
could make up, but the one Hanauer got that day beat them all. The
staff cook, extremely agitated, told Hanauer that water kept shooting up out of the floor drain and splashing up all over the ceiling.

"That's impossible," Hanauer responded. "The inmates are
lying to you."

"I saw it myself," the cook retorted. "The water shot up out
of the drain like a geyser, hit the ceiling, and went everywhere. It
lasted for quite a while."

We had had a lot of trouble with the kitchen drains because
the inmate kitchen help would attempt to unplug them with

broom handles and just end up plugging them up worse. This would cause water to come up out of another floor drain, but not in a violent eruption. The kitchen staff had been after us for quite a while to fix the problem, and Hanauer thought this was an obvious ploy for our attention.

Hanauer continued to tell the cook it was impossible for water to come up out of the drain like he was describing it and called the cook everything from a dirty rotten liar to a staggering drunk. But the cook continued to insist that the drain had become Old Faithful.

Finally, in disgust, Hanauer left and went down to the kitchen dock area immediately below the drain and began questioning workers there. He found out that the inmates in the kitchen had accidentally punched a hole through the bottom of a trap in the main dining room with their broomsticks. This hole had been leaking water onto the inmates working on the dock area.

These wet inmates had called the kitchen and asked them not to allow any more water to go down the drain until it could be fixed. When the leak had continued, the dock area inmates had called again. When that call was also to no avail, the irritated inmates stuck a fire hose up in the drain and turned the water on. In fact, they had done that twice.

Well, Hanauer laughed himself silly and felt kind of bad about the way he had talked to the cook. Not bad enough to apologize to him or even let him know that he had been right after all. In fact, knowing Hanauer, he probably didn't feel bad at all.

And I guarantee he didn't let it hurry him when the plumbing shop got its next emergency call.

Chapter 6

Walls Ain't All That's Dense Around Here

Before I worked at the pen, I didn't realize how awkward grown men could be with basic tools. Growing up on a farm, I had used tools from the time I was small. I could take the wheel off my bike, take out the inner tube, patch it, and put it all back together again when I was eight years old. I could use a shovel and pick, dig a hole, and move the outhouse by the time I was ten, and when I was twelve, I could take the carburetor off the tractor, clean it, and put it back on. By the time I was fourteen, I could take the carburetor off the tractor, clean it, and put it back on, and the tractor would still run. Dad was pleased with this improvement.

I was amazed to find that many of the inmates I first supervised had never even picked up a tool—although I must admit, the labor crew inmates were not exactly the cream of the crop. No one wanted to be on the labor crew; it was the worst work and the lowest paid in all of maintenance. At that time, all prisoners got $6.50 of credit each month to spend in the canteen, which carried such items as street clothes, cigarettes, snacks, magazines, and other common convenience store offerings. Inmates on the labor crew earned a total of $7.50 a month, so the inmate who watched TV all day long in his cell got just one dollar less than the inmate who spent eight hours doing manual labor. Other maintenance shops, such as plumbing and carpentry, paid in the range of ten dollars to fifteen dollars a month, with a couple of positions offering twenty dollars. One lucky inmate would be assigned as the twenty-four-hour man, meaning he was on call twenty-four hours a day should his help be needed. For that, he might earn thirty dollars. Workers in the factories earned even more, starting at fifty dollars a month and going up from there.

Along with better pay, other work assignments attracted inmate workers with opportunities to learn a trade and, most enticing of all, to participate in a related hustle. Laundry workers might charge other inmates to press their clothes or to manage not to "lose" an inmate's street clothes. Laundry workers would also sell clothes "lost" from their owners. In the maintenance shops, inmate workers (especially the twenty-four-hour men) would charge to get work done more quickly than could be achieved going through regular channels. Kitchen workers swiped food to sell.

But there was no hustle for labor crew inmates and no other special draw to get an inmate to ask to be a laborer. The authorities decided where an inmate could work based on his behavior, and when an inmate was assigned to maintenance, the supervisor in charge of inside maintenance would interview him to see if he belonged in one of the shops. If an inmate had no skills, didn't want to learn anything, had a surly disposition, or was a known troublemaker, then he was put on the labor crew, which was usually run by the most inexperienced person in the engineering department. In 1984 that last description, along with words like *nervous*, *gullible*, and *ignorant*, pretty well described me.

One time, I took some of these labor crew inmates with me to dig up a pipe for the plumbing crew and discovered the labor crew inmates honestly could not use a shovel. They didn't have a clue. They tried to stab it, shove it, and kick it into the ground. They even jumped up and down on it. I explained that when the ground is hard and full of rocks, it is necessary to use the pick to loosen up the ground. They argued with me, telling me that you only use a pick to dig through solid rock. When they finally admitted defeat and gave up on the shovels, one of them swung the pick so hard it got stuck in the ground and he couldn't pull it loose. They all gathered around and pulled on the handle until they broke it. Then they smirked among themselves about this stupid square man who thought you could use a pick in that kind of ground.

The one and only good thing about being on the labor crew was the chance to drive the labor truck. Every member of the crew wanted to be the truck driver, not only because it was a chance to drive a vehicle—a rare privilege indeed for someone locked up inside a maximum-security institution—but also because the driver received an extra $2.50 in tips each month. In applying for this coveted position, the inmates would tell me what great drivers they were, and I was surprised at how many of them had driven a dump truck for an uncle before incarceration.

The labor truck was a banged-up, old short-bed Chevy with a clutch and a four speed on the floor. Every day, we'd use the truck to deliver ice (hauled in sawed-off metal barrels) all over the pen, to the housing units and to boxes attached to water fountains in the exercise yards. The labor crew convicts would load as much ice as possible on my little truck, sometimes stacking barrels four or five high. Such loads, combined with inmate drivers who apparently had driven nothing but dump trucks with automatic transmissions, resulted in the occasional load of ice sliding out of the back of the little Chevy. This happened especially down by Two Gate, where the little truck with its worn-out clutch bucked and jumped up the hill after we had stopped to open the gate.

Soon after I was promoted to a maintenance supervisor in the plumbing shop, the new labor supervisor let a convict driver run the truck off down the hill in front of M&M and into a large fence post, thus ending my poor old truck's distinguished career with the Department of Corrections. It was retired without fanfare. The labor supervisor was astonished and later told me, "I thought he'd be a better driver. You know that guy used to drive a dump truck for his uncle in St. Louis?"

When I arrived in the plumbing shop, I was disheartened to find that incompetency was not confined to the labor crew. Some of the plumbing inmates were really gifted in mechanical abilities. Others were not. Some of them could not understand the dynamics of why a crescent wrench is made to turn one way, or how to turn a pipe wrench so it will grip a pipe. Some could never learn which way to turn a valve and would turn and grunt and nearly twist a valve off in their attempt to open it by turning it clockwise. When that didn't work, they would put a pipe wrench on the handle and break the valve or the stem. Some couldn't learn which way to thread a pipe together or apart and didn't have the faintest understanding of why it is necessary to use a back-up wrench, even after breaking several pipes. They would study a union forever and never figure out which pieces unscrewed from each other or which way to turn them to get them apart. As my dad would have put it, they couldn't figure out how to pour cow pee out of a boot if you told them the directions were on the heel. (I always thought the best idea was just to stand a little farther from the cow.)

One of the inmates we hired, a guy named Paul, had those kinds of problems, but he tried hard to learn and really wanted to do a good job. I was back in the plumbing shop after a few years of working in the administrative segregation unit of MSP, and George Frank, who had witnessed my mishap with the exploding sewer pipe, had just come back to work at the pen after a five-year absence. We had had quite a turnover in inmate help, as the factories, which paid double or triple as much, had been hiring our help away from us as soon as they saw we had a capable man. Paul had stayed with us thinking we would make him the twenty-four-hour plumber if he stayed longer than anybody else did. But Paul just couldn't learn. I admired his honest effort, but he never learned how to do anything without constant supervision and tore up as much as he fixed. He, however, did not see it that way. To listen to him talk, he knew it all, had done it all, and had nothing left to learn. Finally, he declared himself the twenty-four-hour man, but we disagreed and kept on looking for better help. The longer we went without filling the slot, the more arrogant and domineering he became, behaving as though he was in charge of all the other inmates. Finally, we realized we would have no choice but to get rid of him.

But before we could do that, the sewer pipe from Housing Unit 4 came apart in Tunnel 12 and spilled its vile contents all over the tunnel floor. The braces from under the sewer pipe and several other pipes had rusted out, causing everything to drop about fourteen inches, but only the sewer pipe had completely come apart. We got the other pipes braced up, but there were too many pipes in the way to get to the broken sewer line. At last, I told the guys that unless they could see a better way, someone would have to lie down on their back, slide under the pipes, and hold that one up while another guy on top put a clamp on it. Nobody got very excited about my idea, but no one could come up with any other way to do it. So I told Paul it was his job to climb under. He told me to have one of the other guys do it, that he wasn't going to get down in that [stuff]. I started to tell him to do as he was told when Mike, a rather large solid fellow, said he would do it and proceeded to lie down under the pipes and hold them up. As he did, the guy working from the top to install a new hubless connector couldn't help but knock loose insulation and dirt down into Mike's face.

When we got back to M&M, I asked Paul to come with me to the office while the others went down to the plumbing shop. I let him know that I was going to let him go but I wasn't going to write him up. He argued that he was the best man we had and that he was the only one who knew what he was doing. I refrained from telling him what I really thought and tried to remind him how hard we had tried to teach him and said that his refusal to do what I told him was the last straw. He finally

A view inside Tunnel 12. These are the pipes that Neal's crew had to fix and that led to the fight between prisoners Paul and Mike.

accepted it and then asked if he could at least go down and get his clothes before he left. I told him there was no problem with that, and as he headed down the stairs, I started filling out the paperwork to lay him in.

At the foot of the stairs was the door to the tool room. Paul walked in and picked up the largest combination wrench we had. Then he went into the plumbing shop, walked up behind Mike, and swung the wrench at his head. Paul's target caught a glimpse of the wrench coming out of the corner of his eye and ducked, so the wrench only glanced off his shoulder. As Paul tried to swing again, Rich, another plumbing inmate, grabbed Paul from behind, pinning his arms. The two of them fell to the floor kicking, grunting, and sweating. Mike was screaming, "I'm gonna kill you!" and was kicking at, and then trying to stomp Paul's head into the concrete. In doing so, he kicked Rich in the eye, but Rich continued to hold on to Paul.

Frank, who'd been looking for an opening into the melee, somehow got the wrench from Paul. He then turned to see that Mike had picked up a short piece of pipe and was coming to finish Paul off. Frank got between them, and Mike backed off, still screaming and threatening, but now mostly for show. I was still upstairs, just finishing my paperwork, and was surprised to see a bunch of officers rush in the front door and down the steps. I followed them down and saw blood on the floor, and Paul and Mike in handcuffs. Paul had a lot of blood on his head, and Rich was busy explaining his part in the episode, hoping that he would not get locked up. Frank was defending him, telling the lieutenant that Rich had probably helped to keep somebody from getting killed. The inmate working in the tool room was telling me that he hadn't thought anything about Paul coming in and getting a tool. It was not unusual for one of the workers to do so, and he had known nothing about what had happened in the tunnel or about me firing Paul.

Rich went on to become our twenty-four-hour plumber and kept the coveted spot for a couple of years, until he and another inmate were caught sharpening a shank on the concrete floor of the parts room. Rich explained to me that he wasn't sharpening it himself, but this other guy was too dense to understand how it was done, so after Rich explained it three times, he decided to risk showing him. He told me that he just couldn't believe how stupid some people are. I could certainly agree with him there. He only reinforced what I had already discovered: Inside a prison, good help is hard to find.

Chapter 7

The Old-Timer's Triumph

Victor was sitting on a cell floor in Housing Unit 3-B. A tough, old weight-lifting convict, he was working on the bolts of a toilet that we needed to pull to replace a leaking wax ring. The inmate who lived in the cell asked Victor if he would like a cup of coffee. Victor told him he could sure use one, so the guy began heating a cup of water. Victor kept on working, and I watched the inmate brew the coffee. He set it down, Victor thanked him, and the hospitable inmate dodged out to visit while he could.

"Vic," I said, "I wouldn't drink that coffee if I were you."

I had never known Victor to pass up a cup of coffee, good or bad. He swiveled around so he could look at me.

"Why not?" he asked. "He's all right, or do you know something that I don't?"

"Well, I watched him make it. He boiled the water, then dipped the coffee in it until it was the right color."

Victor just shrugged his shoulders, asking, "So what?"

I opened the guy's locker, pointed to a nasty, moldy sock, stained a gruesome splotchy black, and said, "This is what he dipped it with."

Victor's face showed a medley of emotions, from curiosity, surprise, and shock to disgust and loathing. He started to dump the coffee into the sink, but I reminded him that the sink would drain into the toilet, and as he had just pulled the toilet away from the wall, the coffee would run out onto the floor. We could hear the inmate coming back down the walk, so Victor began frantically looking around the floor where he was sitting.

"Man, what am I gonna do with this coffee?" I don't think "coffee" was the word he used, but that was what he meant. "Where's his trash can? What can I dump this into?" The inmate stopped at the next cell to gab, giving Victor a chance to jerk the toilet farther from the wall and do his best to throw the coffee into the sewer pipe. He then set the coffee cup on the TV stand.

A cell in Housing Unit 3. The blanket curtain was contraband, but the other items were allowed.

When the guy came back in and saw the empty cup, he quickly volunteered to make Victor another. Victor politely declined.

"Was it okay?"

"Yeah, it really was. It really hit the spot. I appreciate it, homie. I just don't need any more right now."

"Hey, man, I don't mind. I'll go ahead and make some more. You'll want more before you leave. I really appreciate you guys getting here and fixing this for me. It's been a mess in here, mopping up all the time."

"No. No, dog, don't make any more. I've had all I want. Believe me, I couldn't drink another cup."

Finally accepting Victor's decline, the guy left the cell to do some more visiting, and Victor bent back to the task at hand, but I could hear him grumbling.

"What's the matter, Victor?" I asked. "Just wishing you could get a cup of coffee?"

"No. But I was just sitting here thinking. If I'm not mistaken, I got a cup of coffee from that dude last week." He looked at me for a moment, without really seeing me, shook his head, and went back to work, still muttering to himself.

Victor had one of the best how-I-ended-up-in-prison stories I ever heard. He had a girlfriend who had been a hooker and was running a brothel. Victor liked spending time there, and she introduced him to cocaine, for which he quickly developed an addiction. His girlfriend had a daughter who lived with her, and Victor became Uncle Vic to the little girl. He also made friends with her cat, Kitty Cat.

Eventually, Victor's cocaine habit cost him more than he was making, and his girlfriend suggested that he pull off a robbery somewhere. She told him it couldn't be too hard for someone as smart as him and suggested that he think of a place that took in a lot of money, that was familiar to him, and that he could rob without too much chance of getting caught.

He thought of her place.

With most of her money coming from drugs and girls, he didn't think she would get the police involved, and he had no qualms about robbing his own girlfriend. "She's the one that got me started on drugs, she ought to be the one paying for it," is how he justified it to me.

Victor got a friend to help and explained that the friend would have to do all of the talking because they would recognize Victor's voice. So with a couple of ski masks on, they "hit the joint." Everything was going as planned except that the cat kept rubbing up against his leg. Then the little girl said, "That's Uncle Vic, Mom. Why would Uncle Vic rob us?" Victor, keeping his mouth shut, kept kicking at the cat, but it kept coming back to rub on his legs. Then the girl said, "Look, Mama! Even Kitty Cat knows that's Uncle Vic. Why is Uncle Vic robbing us? Doesn't he love us anymore?" As soon as he left, Mama called the cops and told them she had been robbed and that she knew who had robbed her.

When it went to court, Victor's lawyer was confident the prosecution would fail. "Don't worry," he told Victor, "they don't have a case against you. I'll get you off. No problem. We can beat them."

The woman took the stand and testified that she knew it was Victor when he walked in. As she testified, Victor's lawyer leaned over and said, "Don't worry. No problem. She couldn't see your face. I'll ruin her testimony. We can beat her."

Then the little girl took the stand and said she knew it was Uncle Vic who robbed them and she didn't know why he would do that. Victor's lawyer leaned over and said, "No problem. Don't worry. This isn't good and the jury likes her, but I'll get her to say that she never saw your face and discredit her testimony. We can beat her."

Then the little girl said, "Even Kitty Cat knew it was Uncle Vic. Kitty loves Uncle Vic and kept rubbing his leg even when he tried to kick her."

The lawyer leaned over and said, "Your goose is cooked. There is no way we can beat Kitty Cat."

——|–|–|——

I always liked working with Victor, and I was even with him when I had my most memorable MSP meal. I wasn't expecting a meal when we headed to the kitchen. Victor had told me we needed to go there and work on the plumbing. At first, I told him we weren't going as I had just been there and hadn't been

informed of any problems, but he finally convinced me that we
really needed to go. When we got there, we tightened a faucet,
and then we were each offered a plate of food by one of the
Cuban inmate cooks. MSP had seen an influx of Cuban inmates
in the late eighties, and some had ended up working in the main
kitchen. With "leftover" food, these inmates could cook up a
gourmet meal. Victor and I went to work on our heaping plates,
and I discovered it was the best meal I had ever had at the prison
and was better than many I'd had elsewhere.

While we were eating, another inmate kitchen worker came
up with a half gallon of ice cream that had about a spoonful taken
out, and asked Victor if he thought we could eat it, as it would
just get thrown away if we didn't. Victor told him he thought we
could handle it. As soon as he was gone, another came up with a
gallon of peaches that was missing about a cupful and wondered
if we wanted that, too. Victor told him we would get rid of it.

"Vic," I asked, when the other inmate left, "what are we
going to do with all of this food? We can't get all of this back to
the shop."

He smiled and said, "We're going to eat it."

He was serious. And we did. It took us the best part of an
hour, but there was not a drop of ice cream or a slice of peach
left. We even finished off all the peach juice as a topping for the
ice cream. Looking back on it later, I realized that several debts to
Victor were probably paid off with that meal. I know he sure felt
satisfied. As we were waddling back down the main corridor, he
began to chuckle. He patted his belly and said, "That judge that
put me in here thought he was punishing me. I bet he'd be one
mad bugger if he could see me now."

Chapter 8

Push-Ups and Snakes

Mornings in the MSP plumbing shop followed a comfortable routine. Neither Ed Hanauer nor Richard Baumann saw fit to get the inmates to work until coffee was made, the fat was chewed, the merits of Ford cars and trucks were expounded by Hanauer, the latest races and racecar drivers were discussed, and Hanauer had finished bragging about his daughter and his horses.

During this time, the inmates would change into work clothes and settle into a quick game of hearts or dominoes, or start a game of chess that could go on for days (the shop had a unique set of chessmen made from one-quarter-inch and three-eighth-inch plumbing parts). The games would also come out at the end of the day as the inmates waited their turns for the shower. There was always a goodly amount of banter, challenges, and bets on who would win. These bets were normally for push-ups, collectable anytime and anywhere. Many times, I stopped on the way to a job to let one of my workers collect ten or twenty push-ups from a fellow inmate, sometimes in a housing unit or on the upper yard.

The inmates were always trying to get the square men to bet for the fun of making us do push-ups or to razz us if we reneged. One day, as I was waiting for the last of the inmates to finish showering in the afternoon, I sat down at an old workbench and began stacking the dominoes on their ends, one on top of the other. I could stack them about eight high before the tower would topple. When one inmate, Carlos, got out of the shower, he watched me for a few minutes.

"See how high I can get them?" I asked. "Now that takes a steady hand."

A young good-natured guy, Carlos was up to the challenge. "I could stack them higher than that," he retorted. "That's easy."

"I'll bet you can't even stack them up to eight high," I said and moved out of the way. He tried a couple of times, and the dominoes fell when he got them four or five high.

"See," I said, "you can't even get them six high; you'd never get past seven."

"I'll bet you fifty push-ups that I can," he boasted.

"Okay. I'll take that bet. But right now, you need to get back to the cell house. You can try in the morning."

As Carlos left, Hanauer, who had been watching us, started laughing.

"He'll probably come down tomorrow and do it on his first try. Then what'll you do?"

"I only bet on a sure thing," I answered. And then I proceeded to cut some small pieces of wood and put them under the back legs of the table. Next I tried to stack dominoes on the just unlevel surface. It was impossible to go any higher than five high.

The next morning Carlos was all set to try, but I tried to scare him off with a warning.

"Now, Carlos, it's harder than you think. I'll let you out of the bet, if you want."

He laughed, sure I was fearing imminent humiliation.

"Oh, no, Neal. I'm going to do this."

"I'm telling you, Carlos, it's going to be much more difficult than you expect, and no practice tries."

I thought that would deter him, and then I would show him how I had blocked up one side of the table, but my insistence just bolstered his confidence all the more. He sat down and started, and at about three high, the dominoes fell.

Astonished, Carlos blurted out, "Double or nothing! Double or nothing! You've got to give me a chance to win them back!"

"You had better quit now or you'll get in too deep," was my sage advice. "I really don't think you can get them seven high. In fact, I know you can't get them that high. I don't even think I could get them that high today."

Carlos could not be dissuaded. He hunched over the table, bit his tongue, scrunched up his face, and with fierce determination set about stacking the bones. When he got five high, he began to get his confidence back, but the sixth one sent them tumbling.

"One more chance. I'll get them next time. I almost had them that time."

"Carlos," I said, "I really think you ought to give up. You already owe me a hundred pushups, and as fat and clumsy as you are, it'll take a month to work off that debt."

"Double or nothing, one more time. I'll get them this time."

What could I do? Being the feeling, compassionate person that I am, I gave him another chance. And another, and another, and another.

When a bet starts at fifty and gets doubled, and doubled again and again, it adds up in a hurry. Before he knew what happened, Carlos owed me thirty thousand pushups. I could see that he really did need to get in shape, so I kindly began collecting immediately. Ten or fifteen push-ups at a time five or six times a day, with Carlos griping and complaining all the time that I was trying to kill him and was inflicting cruel and unusual punishment. At the same time, he admitted several times that he was glad someone was making him exercise because he wanted to work out but couldn't make himself do it.

Besides getting him in shape, that huge debt also meant I was free to bet him push-ups without having to risk him collecting, and we bet on everything. I wanted to give him the chance to get back even because I really felt bad about blocking up the table legs. Well, that's not really true. I was kind of pleased with myself for the way I had conned him, but I did feel obligated to give him the opportunity to get some of the push-ups back. It was too bad for him because no matter what we bet on, he couldn't win. I was collecting sixty or seventy push-ups each day, and yet his debt was growing. I even let him bet as much as a couple of thousand on what should have been sure things, and he would still lose.

Before long, Carlos had muscles popping out on his arms, neck, and chest, and he got to where he could do fifty push-ups at a time. I didn't even have to ask for them. He'd come into the shop, drop to the floor and do fifty each morning, after lunch, and before he went in at the end of the day. Things might have gone on like this forever, but I was reassigned to a maintenance post in the Special Management Facility and had to find new inmates to aggravate. Fortunately, I have a talent for just that sort of thing.

About a year later, Housing Unit 5, with 5-A and 5-B, was changed to protective custody. Inmates who needed protection from other inmates could check themselves in or be checked in by administration. It was a prison unto itself. "Population inmates," those not in protective custody, did not come into contact with inmates checked into protective custody in SMF. It wasn't long after the change that Carlos checked in. SMF maintenance hired him back, and the fun started again.

At that time, the SMF maintenance office was in the 5-C building, and Louie Markway was the maintenance supervisor in charge. Carlos was always doing something that would aggravate Markway. Then Markway found out that Carlos hated snakes. *Hate* is too mild a word. Carlos despised snakes; he couldn't even stand to talk about snakes. It was torture for him to think about snakes. So Markway brought in this very lifelike two-foot-long rubber snake, and we began to learn how high Carlos could jump, how fast he could run, and that he could jump in the air in one direction and then run in a different direction before he even came back down.

Now I wouldn't want to give you the idea that Markway was a real sadistic kind of guy, but Carlos had pushed about as much as Markway could take, and it was payback time. Every time Carlos would open a toolbox or a desk drawer, he'd jump, cuss, and run, and Markway would laugh until he was gasping for air. Markway even hid the snake in the bathroom, and Carlos proved that while it's not easy to run with your britches down around your ankles, it can be done. After a couple of weeks, though, Carlos got used to the gag, and the best Markway could get from him was a twinge or quick jerk. So the snake got put away, and Carlos tried not to aggravate any more than he felt obligated to. He did, however, still do one thing that Markway didn't like.

When Carlos would come back from lunch, he would sit in a chair in front of Markway's desk, put his feet on the desk, and rock his chair back on two legs. Markway felt that this was disrespectful, but he hated to tell Carlos to quit after all he had done to him. He did suggest to him that he not do it, but that only encouraged Carlos to keep it up. Finally, I came up with a plan that I shared with Markway, and he gave me the go-ahead.

The shop had no regular ceiling, just pipes, ductwork, conduit, and the like. I tied a string to a piece of cardboard and slid it, with the rubber snake lying on top of it, onto the duct work just over the chair where Carlos liked to sit. Then I ran the string around the corner over a pipe and back to where I would sit.

After Carlos came in, propped up his feet, and leaned his chair back, I began to tell Markway a story of something that really had happened to my wife when she was about fourteen.

"The old wooden country church where Diana went as a young girl had a small front porch with no ceiling, so the short rafters and joists were exposed. She took her baby cousin out onto the porch one Sunday night because the baby kept crying. Diana noticed something dark starting to drip out of the ceiling and looked up just in time to see a large black snake falling down towards the baby. She only had time to hold the baby away from her, so the snake dropped through her arms, between her and the baby, and fell on the porch. Diana started screaming and dancing all over that snake and then ran back into the church."

As I told the story Carlos's eyes had gotten bigger and bigger, and when I finished he said in a quiet, awed voice, "I would have died! I would have died right then!"

That was when I pulled the string.

I had it fixed so the string held the cardboard up, but the snake fell right into Carlos's lap. Now you talk about screaming and dancing. He couldn't get out of the chair or away from the snake. It sat on his fat little belly, bouncing up and down, wiggling and jiggling and threatening to bite him at every move. Finally, the chair had had enough, and Carlos, with arms waving, legs pumping, and eyes popping out of their sockets, went over backwards. The snake went up into the air, and Carlos went down onto the floor. He proceeded to do the backstroke as the snake, like a living thing, aimed itself at his head. About the time it landed, Carlos shuddered, gasped, and froze with the snake curled around his face. I swear that the snake was grinning. Markway was in the floor gasping for breath and holding his belly. His position was much like Carlos's, but emotionally they were worlds apart.

When he had finally composed himself, Carlos got up. He kicked the snake, kicked the chair, kicked the desk, and thought about kicking Markway, then thought better. He still didn't understand how we had done it. He never again put his feet on the desk, and every time he went by it, he would glance at the ceiling and hurry on past. All in all, I would have to admit it was one of my greatest successes, but from that time on, Carlos never gave me another push-up. Somehow he figured he had paid his debt.

Chapter 9

Plungers Are Weapons Too

Have you ever seen an inmate wearing a short homemade dress, dancing on a table, and singing, "Quack, quack! I'm a duck! I can't play dominoes worth—" Never mind just how the song goes; I have seen it and it wasn't a pretty sight.

It all started with Ed Hanauer, of course. Unable to leave well enough alone, he encouraged the inmates to get more creative in their betting instead of sticking to push-ups; then, when a bet was perhaps a little more than someone was willing to risk, he'd soup them up by asking, "Why? Are you expecting to lose? You're a chicken [poop]!" or "Come on be a man! Don't be afraid."

Most of the older cons had been around too long to fall for that kind of badgering, but the new kids always had something to prove. During the time he worked in the plumbing shop, Hanauer was probably responsible for doubling the size of check-in. Many times, before the bet was taken, there had to be an agreement that the bet could only be collected in the privacy of the plumbing shop area. That did not keep the machine shop, also in the basement of the M&M building, from being notified when a particularly interesting bet was about to be collected.

One of the bets that became popular for a while was for losers to do a song and dance. That consisted of a shuffling of the feet, a clapping of the hands, and a rendition of the "Quack, quack! I'm a duck!" song in a high, quiet, embarrassed voice. It was usually done as quickly as possible to beat the crowd of spectators rushing over from the machine shop. Seldom did the dancer finish quickly enough. It's an amazing sight to see some time-hardened, rough, old convict, red-faced and humiliated as a crowd gathered at the plumbing shop door to cheer and whistle.

One day, tough old Victor lost to a new inmate named Brian who was full of spit and vinegar. Brian was one of those guys who couldn't back down from any bet. For Victor to have to do the song and dance was bad enough, but to lose to a snotty-nosed little smart aleck was unthinkable. The good-natured mood of the shop started to get ugly when the youngster began to crow about how great he was and how he would surely be recognized now as the king of the domino players. About that time, Rivers, the inmate who had been disgusted with my eagerness to attend to plumbing "emergencies," suggested that Victor and Brian play another game and added that the bet should include a striptease on the workbench. The loser would don a skimpy dress to strip off while singing the old song, "Quack, Quack."

Victor shot Rivers a hard look. Everyone except the new kid knew that it had only been luck that he had won twice, but Victor realized that luck can be a tough opponent to beat. Seeing his hesitation, the kid expressed his willingness to make the bet and began his obnoxious boasting that the old man was afraid because he knew that he'd get beaten again.

Victor gave Rivers another hard look, which seemed to say, "If I lose I'll have to kill this kid, then I'll have to kill you for causing it." Then he agreed to the bet. The kid's luck had run out. After losing the game, he tried to weasel out of the bet, saying he would do the song and dance, but as they had no dress, he couldn't do the striptease. The other guys told him not to worry, they would find one. The next few days he came to work pretty nervous, but as nothing more was said about it for about a week, he relaxed and began to be his old, obnoxious self. Then one day he was handed a piece of cloth and asked to try it on.

Sudden realization drained the color from his face, and he made a wild dash for the door. He could not escape; the way was blocked by not only all of the guys from the machine shop but also several from shops upstairs. The kid was given the option of putting on the dress or having it put on for him. His hopeless answer was to again dash at the door.

I expressed concern at the turn of events, but Hanauer assured me the crowd wouldn't get too rough. After a few moments of useless struggle, the kid gave up, and the others put the dress on him and set him on the table. Then, to the whoops and whistles of the crowd, he did the quickest song and dance on record. He was not required to do the striptease and was in fact defended by the rest of the plumbing crew when some of the other spectators demanded an encore. The kid had settled his debt and won a measure of respect from the rest of the shop. He put up enough fight to be respected, but he gave in and paid up when it was time to do it.

He went on to become one of our better workers and learned how to get along with people, but to the best of my recollection, he never, ever bet on anything else again.

Another time it wasn't Victor but me who was chafing under the boasting of a domino opponent. One morning, a big, friendly black inmate known as Moose got the best of me in a game. There had been no betting, but Moose was still strutting and bragging all around the plumbing shop. After suffering in silence for a few minutes, I noticed the plunger that the inmates used for washing out clothes in the sink, and I got an idea.

Moose had just had his head shaved. It wasn't exactly the look he'd wanted. Just for laughs, he'd first gotten a Mr. T haircut (a Mohawk), but the administration didn't see the humor in his new do. In fact, they told him he was trying to incite racial unrest and demanded that he get rid of it. Now there is only one way to get rid of a Mr. T haircut. Luckily, the administration didn't have a problem with Michael Jordan or Moose would have had to get rid of that style too, and we would have had to draw some hair on his head with a magic marker.

Eyeing Moose's slick, shiny top, I grabbed the plunger, snuck up behind him, and plopped it down on his head. My intention was to jerk it back off and see how loud the pop would be. I was sure that would change the shop's topic of conversation.

To my surprise, the plunger stuck tight, and my jerking only caused Moose to stagger backwards with arms flailing as he tried to keep his balance. I jerked harder, sure it would come off with a hard pull, and he again staggered backward, arms flapping about in the air and his eyes wide with fear as he wondered what in tarnation had grabbed him by the head so tightly that it could drag him around.

It should've been funny, but I wasn't laughing. I was beginning to fear I'd given Moose a new permanent accessory. I jerked again, using all my strength, and once again Moose lurched backward. But this time, he lost his footing and fell to the floor with a weak cry. As he fell, the plunger finally came loose with a loud *pop!* I looked at the crowd of inmates who had witnessed my triumph, and they were literally rolling on the floor, laughing and gasping for breath. Hanauer and Baumann both were wiping tears from their faces.

I was standing over my victim with the plunger in my hand as he stared up at me in wonder and astonishment, comprehension slowly dawning on him. Suddenly his gaze fastened on the weapon I held, his confusion flashed into horror, and, he cried out, "Oh, no, man! Not a plunger on my head!"

With that, he leaped to his feet and ran to the sink, where he began to scrub his bald head with soap while moaning, "No man, not a plunger on my head!" In between fits of laughter, I tried to tell him it was a clean plunger, the one only ever used to wash clothes, but he just kept splashing his head with water, scrubbing his scalp with soap, and moaning about having a nasty plunger fastened to his head. It was such a funny trick and got such a great response from everyone that I began to stalk the plumbing shop for another victim. I found several likely subjects. Hanauer didn't have much hair, so he watched me pretty closely.

About a week later, Johnny, an inmate from the carpenter shop, walked into the plumbing shop. Johnny was a squirrelly little guy who would do any crazy thing for attention. Just a few days before, he had shaved his head to get a laugh from Ralph Sanders, who ran the carpenter shop upstairs. The still-bald Johnny found his way to the plumbing shop's domino table, and as that was out of bounds for him, I decided he was fair game. I crept up behind him and attached the plunger to the top of his head. He thought it was funny and told me to leave it on so he could go upstairs and show Sanders his new headgear. He disappeared up the stairs, the handle of the plunger wobbling wildly, while he shouted, "Hey! Look at me! Look at me!"

I had forgotten all about him when he reappeared about fifteen minutes later, plunger still attached to his little head. I told him we had better remove it, as it might not be good for him to leave it on that long. I really hadn't thought it would stay on that long without coming loose.

I was a little nervous as I went to take it off, but that nervousness morphed into horror when I saw what the plunger had done. The whole top of Johnny's head was purple and swollen up like a balloon. It also had a ghastly dead-white line sunk down where the edge of the plunger had been. It was the sickest hickey I'd ever seen, and I was sure the top of his head would shrivel and die. How, I thought, will I write up an accident report for killing the top of an inmate's head with a plunger?

Johnny, on the other hand, wasn't the least concerned. As soon as I removed the plunger, he ran to a mirror, broke out in a huge grin, said, "Cool!" and ran off to show Sanders. I kept a nervous watch on him the next few days as the purple turned to black and the swelling slowly subsided. Then I didn't fully relax until his hair grew back and covered his head.

Hanauer's response was to tell me I needed to learn to behave myself and not be pulling stunts on the inmates all the time, but I knew he was just jealous because he'd never top my crowning achievement.

Chapter 10

Bloodshed inside the Walls

I didn't know what to expect when I answered the call that afternoon to go to the tag plant. All I knew was that a wounded officer needed a ride to the MSP Hospital. As I was still the labor supervisor at the time, I was called to pick him up in the M&M truck.

When I went inside, I saw a crazy-eyed inmate holding a square-point shovel. Several staff members were circling him with weapons in hand—the weapons being whatever was handy, from short pieces of two-by-fours to short lengths of pipe. Among the staff members was Captain Gary Blank, who had blood running down one side of his head. I was later informed that the inmate had pulled the shovel out of the ice barrel, come up behind the captain, and struck him on the head with it.

I did not join the circle but stood back. The inmate worked his way around to the back of a forklift and was unwinding a piece of log chain. Another captain arrived and began telling the inmate that he was already in enough trouble and he really didn't want to use that chain. With that, the convict grinned, dropped his weapons, turned around, and put his hands behind his back. After he had been secured and taken out, I got Blank into the truck and took him to see Hamburger Tom. Honest! That was the nickname for the convict medic.

Hamburger Tom, like most inmates back then, had a hustle to make extra money. His hustle was to sew up inmates who had been wounded or cut up in a fight to help them avoid the problems of being linked to a fight, a stabbing in the yard, or a wild melee somewhere in a corridor.

Back in the 1950s and 1960s, MSP had a national reputation for violence. The negative spotlight found MSP after the Great Riot of 1954, in which four inmates were killed and fifty inmates and four officers were injured. Overcrowding was a big problem leading to the inmates' discontent; in A-Hall, for example, six men lived in cells that in the 1980s were allowed to house only two. The next ten years brought many improvements—better inmate education, more freedom of movement, new menus, and less crowding, to name a few—but violence was still high enough to make MSP and its improvement the subject of campaign promises in the 1964 Missouri governor's race.

Even when I arrived in 1984, inmate-on-inmate violence was still a fact of life inside MSP. Stabbings were not unusual, and fights and brawls were common. A regular topic of morning discussions among the inmates was who had gotten stabbed and how badly, or, in some cases, how far the victim had gotten before he died. I saw a few bloody trails in housing units after altercations between inmates had been settled with homemade weapons. I remember very clearly a blood trail down the steps of Housing Unit 4 that ended in a pool of blood where the inmate died before he could reach the sergeant's office. The blood had been mopped up, but it had stained the stone steps and the concrete floor.

At least three to five times each summer there would be instances where tower officers came out on the walks and cut loose with a shotgun round to help quell a disturbance. Summers were hard, especially when the temperature would climb into the nineties for several days in a row. Tempers were short and every aggravation was exaggerated. The stone buildings would retain heat, so the convicts would spend sleepless nights in sweat-drenched bunks, and showers were unavailable until the next evening. By the time the inmates were let out of their cells in the mornings, they were ready to kill the first person who looked cross-eyed at them. (That's one reason you seldom saw cross-eyed inmates.)

Inmates vigorously defended their right to use violence,

and they believed violence was the only way to have any kind of control over their situation as it related to other inmates. More than one inmate explained to me, "If you complain to an officer when someone does something wrong to you, then in the eyes of all convicts you are a snitch and deserve anything they can do to you." Many of the same prisoners who would argue for hours against the state having a right to execute a murderer would, at the same time, defend convicts having the right to kill anyone who stole from them, tried to punk them, or squealed on them to the "cops," meaning prison staff. The difference, it was explained to me, was that a person should have a right to exact retribution on the one who did them wrong, but not the state, as the state was not personally wronged.

I had one conversation with an inmate concerning the death penalty that went something like this:

"What if someone raped, tortured, and murdered your mom?" I asked. "You don't believe they would deserve to die for that?"

"Of course, they would. I would kill them myself."

"But the state shouldn't kill them?"

"No! Someone in the family should."

"But what if you killed the wrong guy? And what about his family? Should they kill you for killing that guy?"

"They ought to try. And if I get the wrong guy, then that's his tough luck. The state can get the wrong guy, too."

"But at least the state has to convince twelve different people who don't even know this guy that he's the one who did it. That would take a lot of evidence, and then there would be all kinds of appeals. They would be less likely to kill the wrong guy than you would."

"I doubt it, and any guy that I would kill would deserve it anyway. That's all nonsense, anyway. The fact is if the state kills anyone, it's murder. They never have the right to do it."

——|—|—|——

Several of the officers I knew back then showed me scars on their hands and arms that were made by a convict yielding a home-made shank. I was also told the story of how Corrections Officer Walter Farrow was killed in July 1979. I have actually been told several versions of how it happened, and the following is, I think, the closest to the truth.

Farrow worked in the vegetable room, just off the kitchen dock. Back then, the inmates working in that area were issued untethered knives to peel and slice vegetables and fruit in food preparation. These were real kitchen knives, not just paring knives. One of the inmates who worked in the vegetable room, Bobby Lewis Shaw, was promised a diamond ring if he would kill Warden Donald Wyrick. Inmate Shaw was a couple of potatoes shy of a full sack and misunderstood his orders to mean Clinton Wyrick, the warden's uncle and a worker in the commissary. On July 16, 1979, Shaw started towards the door with a knife, and Farrow told him he could not leave until he checked the knife back in. Farrow may have thought Shaw was just going to the bathroom. Shaw leaned over the desk and stabbed Farrow—the wound was seven inches deep and pierced his diaphragm and liver—and then Shaw ran out.

Bleeding profusely, Farrow went to the door and ordered Shaw to return. Two other kitchen inmates helped Farrow back to a chair and one of them telephoned for assistance. In the mean-time, Shaw found Clinton Wyrick at his desk in the commissary. Without a word, the inmate approached and began stabbing Wyrick with a butcher knife. Wyrick managed to fend off the attack by kicking with his feet, but his right arm was severely injured, with all of the arteries and ligaments cut as the knife went all the way through. He was also stabbed once in the left arm. The attack lasted between thirty and forty-five seconds and ended with Shaw running out of the commissary.

This was before the installation of the fences that later divided the pen into zones, so Shaw was able to cover a lot of the prison as he was chased around by the custody staff. I've heard that Warden Wyrick yelled up to several of the tower officers to shoot the murderer if he would not stop running, but none of them fired a shot. Finally, Shaw was cornered and captured. He was taken to what is now the major's office and confessed to the investigator, who at that time was Mark Schreiber, a man whose career with MSP began in 1968 and who knows more history and stories about MSP than a museum could hold. (Schreiber, who retired as deputy warden in 2010, later co-authored the book on the Missouri Department of Corrections history: *Somewhere in Time: 170 Years of Missouri Corrections* and authored the pictorial book *Shanks to Shakers: Reflections of the Missouri State Penitentiary.*)

Wyrick barely survived, and Farrow died in the prison hospital from blood loss within an hour of the attack. Shaw was eventually convicted and sentenced to death, but concerns about the sentence in light of his mental defect took the case all the way to the U.S. Supreme Court, which voted five to four against stopping the execution. His execution by injection was set for June 9, 1993, but Missouri Governor Mel Carnahan intervened. Stating that there was little doubt Shaw was mentally unfit for execution, Carnahan commuted Shaw's sentence to life without parole just days before the death sentence was to be carried out.

These tragic events had a lasting impact on MSP. The institution gained several new fences, gates, and locks, and when I went to work there in 1984, it was a common complaint of the maintenance staff that it was impossible to get work done because of all the fences and gates that had to be gone around and unlocked. I was still a bit nervous even with the fences and considered them a good addition to a place infamously called the "bloodiest forty-seven acres in America."

Chapter 11

Turning Up the Heat

"Good news, boys! There's no hot water in Housing Unit 2! You know what that means. It's time to clean the boiler!"

Groans answered Ed Hanauer's announcement. Still in my first week in the plumbing shop, I didn't know what was ahead of us, but I figured if it made Hanauer that cheerful, it had to be bad. After not having much bossing for seven months as a labor supervisor, I was still adjusting to having Hanauer telling me when and what he wanted me to do. It was hard enough just getting used to looking at him, much less letting him give me orders.

The groaning inmates began pointing to Aaron, the new guy on the inmate crew, and proclaiming that he needed to be taught the process of boiler cleaning. Hanauer looked at me with what I would come to know as his have-I-got-a-dirty-job-for-you grin.

"I think Neal needs to learn about boilers, too," he said.

Now I was always looking for opportunities to learn new things, but already Hanauer's glee gave me a sense of foreboding.

The inmates began to gather equipment, and I was a little surprised by their choices. They got hammers, large wrenches, rubber overshoes, shovels, pipe wrenches, water hoses, and a garden rake.

"Do I really need to take all this stuff?" I asked Hanauer.

"The inmates know what they're doing. They're just taking what they need."

"Just how is the water heated?" I asked, baffled and growing more and more wary. I had imagined the boiler would be a tank with a large gas burner, but Hanauer explained that it was a large tank with steam pipes that ran back and forth inside.

"Calcium from the hard water builds up on the pipes after awhile and in effect insulates them so the steam no longer heats the water," Hanauer finished.

"So how do we . . . ?

"Just wait," Hanauer said, knowingly. "You'll see. I'll go with you."

The boiler was located in Tunnel 12. The access door to the tunnel was in a raised concrete structure about five feet square and two feet high. The heavy solid door lay on top and was locked with a Folger Adam key, which I had checked out from the round gate. It took two guys straining to lift the tunnel door open.

One of the inmates stepped over the concrete onto a home-made pipe ladder and descended into the darkness below. We handed down the tools and then followed. Hanauer flipped a couple of light switches, and dim eight-foot-long fluorescent lamps with blackened ends punched a few holes in the gloom. We were in a solid concrete passageway about eight feet high. Though the tunnel was about ten feet wide, we didn't have that much walking space. About three feet of one side were filled floor to ceiling with pipes and conduit resting on a framework. Hanauer pointed out the huge steam and return lines, the eight-inch water supply line, sewer lines, high-voltage conduit, and other various pipes and conduit. There were pools of blackish water on the floor, and piled up under the framework were heaps of old insulation, broken pipes, pieces of brick, glass, fluorescent tube ends, and rotting unidentifiable trash, but where we walked was relatively clear.

We traveled fifty feet, turned a corner, went another 150 feet and came to another gate that had to be opened to follow the tunnel back towards Housing Unit 2. This gate was homemade of metal slats and swung from rusted hinges that cried when forced into use. After the gate, the tunnel narrowed considerably, and strategically placed about halfway between two of the tunnel's lights was a protruding metal rod attached to one of the giant valves on the steam pipe. Contrary to his usual nature, Hanauer warned me about it (probably because he thought I had seen it). As I maneuvered around the hazard, I noticed someone had duct-taped a cap from a spray paint can over the end of the rod.

After two more turns in the tunnel, Hanauer joyfully said, "There she blows!" I looked toward the end of the tunnel and saw nothing to be happy about. Though it was the end of the tunnel as far as walking goes, several of the pipes teed off into two small tunnels that continued on the upper left side. The pipes looked fine, but steam was blowing from an antiquated, dilapidated condensate pump. Beside it was a monstrous prehistoric tank with remnants of some kind of primeval asbestos insulation partially covering but mostly lying under it. Three beat-up fifty-five-gallon barrels decorated the floor, one lying on its side, one filled with some kind of grayish-orange gravel, and one standing empty. The floor had a half inch of greenish water with a skim of oil that reflected the feeble light with an iridescent sheen. There was a metal three-step ladder to climb up into the small tunnels that actually ran under Housing Unit 2. The ladder had four legs and a flat stool-like top. Hanauer quickly grabbed the ladder and, finding a corner that was fairly dry, perched himself upon it and watched the convicts go to work.

Their first steps were to turn off the two-inch steam valves to the tank, put eighteen-inch pipe wrenches on the handles, and crank them down tight. The inmates then opened four-inch valves on the bottom of the tank, and I realized why all of them had put on rubber overshoes. Too late, Rivers told me I should have put some on, too. I had followed Hanauer's example and was in my work boots. I looked at him, balanced high and dry above the swirling flood, and wondered how hard I'd have to bump him to dislodge him from his perch, but I was distracted from this line of thought by an explosion of rats from under the boiler.

The half dozen wet rats were perturbed that their happy little asbestos homes were being flooded, but, I was relieved to see, they were also indisposed to challenge our invasion. Most of the convicts were used to rats, but Aaron had been hanging back, hoping, I think, to keep from being involved in what promised to be an unpleasant job. Unfortunately for him, he was standing right where the rats wanted to go. He thought he was under attack, and with a cry that sounded like a cross between a scream and a whimper— sort of a scrimper— he backed against

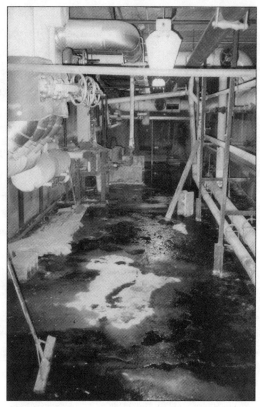

The end of Tunnel 12 under Housing Unit 2. The picture was taken after the boiler was removed and the tunnel was cleaned up, a task that included removing asbestos and installing new lights.

a wall and watched the rats continue down the tunnel until all of them were out of sight.

After letting most of the water out of the tank, the inmates shut off the water going into the boiler. When I asked if it wouldn't have been smarter to have shut off the water before opening the tank, the inmates explained that the running water helped cool down the tank's interior. When the tank was finally empty, the inmates cranked the steam back on and just as quickly turned it back off. They then turned the water back on for a minute before again shutting it off. Hanauer said this helped to pop the calcium deposits off the pipes. Next, the inmates began to remove inspection covers on the back ends of the boiler tank. From his perch, Hanauer warned them to be careful with the gaskets, and the inmates reminded him that they had done this before. When the covers were off, I sloshed over in my wet shoes and looked inside.

The bottom fifteen inches of the tank was full of the same kind of grayish-orange gravel I had seen in the barrel; some chunks as big as half a hollowed softball. The inmates dragged a barrel over to the opening and began to shovel out the gravel. The insides of the tanks were still hot, and the inmates began to sweat and shed clothes. They used the rake to drag as much of the calcium gravel to the front as possible, but eventually the guys had to begin taking turns crawling into the tank to help shovel it out. This was when the inmates used the hose—to spray the inmate inside the boiler to help keep him cool. Inside the boiler, crisscrossing pipes left little room for bodies, so the man inside would roll over onto his back and use a hammer to tap the steam pipes and knock off more of the calcium deposits. He would then use his arms, hands, and feet in an action similar to making snow angels to push the gravel to the back where it could be shoveled out.

Even with the spray from the hose, it was sweltering inside the boiler. This was, in part, because the steam valves didn't hold too well, and a small amount of steam continued to circulate in the pipes. About every ten minutes the inmates would change off. The guy inside would work his way back to the opening until he had his legs sticking out, and then the other guys would pull and lift him out, supporting him until they could stand him up. In spite of all the arguing the inmates had done on the way over regarding who would have to climb inside, no one had to be told to go in; all good workers, the inmates volunteered. Rivers and one other inmate,

Smitty, insisted on being the ones inside the most. Every once in a while, one of the inmates would tell Aaron, who was still hunkered up by the wall, that there weren't any rats in the boiler if he wanted to get inside, and they would laugh when his only response was to glare at them and scrunch up closer to the wall.

The inmates informed me that this was a job that had to be done somewhere in the prison almost every week. There were, in fact, two boilers in the hospital basement, two in the plumbing shop (I had seen them but hadn't realized what they were), three under Housing Unit 5, and two in K-4, just off the kitchen dock. The ones on the kitchen dock did not require the same maintenance because the kitchen had a water softener and the boilers had removable steam bundle tubes. All of the rest had to be climbed into to clean. The hardest ones to get to were the ones we were working on in Tunnel 12 and the boilers in the bottom of the hospital. The ones that had to be done most often were under Housing Unit 5 because these supplied hot water for the laundry in addition to the housing unit.

The guys began to button the tank up, taking extra care with the gasket. We filled it up and checked for leaks, which we found, but they weren't bad enough to concern Hanauer. So we picked up our tools and headed out. On the way, we pried Aaron loose from where he had glued himself to the wall. I asked Hanauer why the stuff we had removed was red if it was just calcium, and he claimed it was the rust in the water mains that caused the discoloration.

Back in the sunshine, I splish-splashed my way back to the shop, my socks and shoes full of water, asbestos, and gravel. I made up my mind to wait for my chance to get even with Hanauer, but that was a lost cause. While I was waiting, Hanauer would always find a dozen new ways to torment me.

Chapter 12

Vats Disgusting

It was all because of the rats. They ate the wax. That was what I finally figured out.

When I started working at the prison, I was not surprised to learn that it had a population of rats; however, I was taken aback by their numbers. The dreaded rodents had found a most accommodating home at MSP. Most of the buildings were old and run-down with lots of cracks and holes through which rats could gain entrance, and there were miles of dark tunnels that provided quiet shelter. But even more enticing to the rats was the endless buffet of garbage the prison provided. The MSP kitchen served more than two thousand meals three times a day. When I began working at the prison, all of the garbage and leftover food was dumped into a huge uncovered vat that sat at the kitchen dock.

The trash company came to swap out the vat a couple of times a week, and in the meantime, the area around the vat would get rank. Before leaving the prison premises with the filled vat, the trash truck would stop in the train gate so officers could jam sharpened rods into the muck to spear anybody who had failed to enjoy prison hospitality as much as we would have liked. Once, two inmates did hide in the nauseating contamination, using tubes from milk bags in cafeteria dispensers as snorkels. The sweat-stained officer who punched holes in the slop that day failed to adequately fulfill his mission, and the unpunctured inmates sloshed out to freedom.

The inmates had planned their escape with a female accomplice. She had driven her car behind the slop bucket as it left the prison a few times to familiarize herself with its route out of town to the dump. She had told the inmates to jump out at the fourth stop, where she would be waiting with an escape vehicle. On the chosen day, however, the normal truck driver didn't show up, so the trash company sent another driver, and the other driver decided to take a different route. When the fourth stop came, the slimy, stinking inmates jumped out of the goo and landed in the middle of a subdivision. Gagging and seasick, the men found no ride and nowhere to hide.

Someone on the street who had witnessed the men's incredible emergence alerted the police. The reeking men were not hard to track; neither was it difficult for the police to know they had found the right men. The main problem was finding an officer willing to arrest them because no one wanted to have to haul the escapees back in his patrol car. Finally, the officers called MSP. At first, prison officials refused to believe that anyone could be gone, but when the situation was explained, they sent a couple of prison officers to bring the men back.

That escapade had happened in the 1970s, a few years before I began working at the prison. I had a hard time imagining a level of desperation that would drive a man to hide in the fermenting, putrid garbage. I found just getting close to the kitchen dock was, on some days, enough to make me gag.

Rats, however, took a different view, and each night hundreds, if not thousands, of rats took advantage of the vat's offerings. In fact, if there had not been rats willing to pitch in and do their part, we probably would have needed to empty the garbage vat four or five times a week, which would've cost the state several thousand dollars more each year.

While the rats did their best to remain out of sight during the day, there were times when the people who lived and worked inside MSP were inconsiderate enough to disturb them. Once the refrigeration crew went up to the major's office, removed a window air conditioner, and carried it down to a worktable in the refrigeration shop. When they removed the outer cover, a rat jumped out. It was hard to tell who was the most frightened, the rat or the inmates. As the rat jumped down from the worktable, the inmates scattered. One jumped up on the workbench, knocking over the major's air conditioner. It hit the floor with a crash, little pieces flew in all directions, and with a hiss and a long, low moan, the unit expired.

Now the inmates were really scared. The rat had startled them, but killing the major's air conditioner *terrified* them. Feverishly, they began grabbing parts and examining the twisted remains of the appliance with the futile hope of putting it all back together again. The refrigeration foreman called the major and explained that a rat had gotten into the unit and had eaten and destroyed so much that it was beyond repair. The inmates waited, holding their breath, to see if the major would want to come down and see the rat destruction for himself, but he was only interested in getting another air conditioner. Hopefully, a rat-proof one.

The reign of the rats at MSP declined with the arrival of the monsters—Muffin Monsters, that is, giant garbage disposals that were installed in the food service areas. The Muffin Monsters allowed the garbage to go into the sewer system and thus eliminated the need for the garbage vat at the kitchen dock (and one opportunity for inmates to get out before we could properly say our goodbyes). The new garbage solution also led to sudden famine for the legions of rats that had been so fat and happy under the previous arrangement. These rats grew ever braver in their search for nourishment and much less discriminating in their eating habits.

Along about that time I was working in the Special Management Facility, the secure area that included Housing Units 5-A, 5-B, and Supermax, and we began to have a rash of leaking toilets in Supermax. The lockdown unit had nice big plumbing closets between the cells, and the tunnel area doubled as the return air duct, which meant there was a grill on the closet walls shared with the cells. The inmates, always eager for a break in their monotonous existence, could talk to me through this grill while I worked. A few of the inmates had even managed to take the grills out and get into the plumbing closet. But there was nowhere for them to go from there, so they vented their frustration by tearing up the plumbing.

As I began to repair the leaking toilets, I found that the problem wasn't just wax rings that weren't sealing, but wax rings that had disappeared. While I knew inmates could get into the plumbing tunnel, the missing wax rings still left me scratching my head (not literally, for I had found that was not a wise thing to do when changing wax rings; plumbers also learn not to bite their fingernails). Why, I wondered, would inmates go to all of the trouble of breaking into a tunnel just to scratch off a wax ring that would then send sewer water leaking into their cells? It didn't make sense to me, but then neither did a lot of the behavior of bored convicts.

Finally, on about the fifth repair job involving missing rings, I noticed tiny claw marks and it dawned on me. It wasn't the inmates. The rats did it. The rats had eaten the wax rings right off the backs of the toilets. We discovered later that they had also eaten all of the plastic air lines that were part of the pneumatic controls for the heating and air conditioning for the whole building, and we lost all control of the heating, ventilation, and air conditioning until contractors came in and replaced everything, a job that cost the state about $50,000. I guess the rats figured the state still owed them for their earlier garbage disposal services. Actually, we were going to have to replace the control system anyway because the air system had become saturated with oil from a bad air compressor. Many times I pictured some poor half-starved rat biting into his supper of plastic spaghetti only to be assaulted by a blast of oil-laden air. Talk about adding insult to injury.

Still, the remains of the tubing indicated the rats found the plastic air lines to be better than nothing. No doubt they, like the prisons' human residents, had come to the realization that prison food might not be especially tasty but it is at least filling, even if it is full of surprises.

Chapter 13

Digging in the Pen

"Hey, Neal, watch this."

I looked up at Rivers. We were standing by the fence between the gym and the vocational-technical building, which would later become Eight-Dorm. Rivers stuck a shovel in the rain-softened ground, and then, with his hand and foot on the shovel, he reached out and grabbed the chain link fence. I watched in amazement as his shoulder-length hair drifted out from his head and stood on its ends.

"How did you do that?" I asked as I reached for the fence. I felt a sharp tingle, and the hair on my arms lifted.

"It works better if you're holding onto something that's stuck in the ground. The electrical service under the ground is leaking."

"Leaking? What do you mean it's leaking?" I asked. "Electricity doesn't leak—it shorts out to ground. And," I added, mystified, "it wouldn't short out to ground and come back up a shovel just to go back down to ground."

Rivers just grinned at me as he put his hand back on the fence, and his hair stood out from his head.

"It's 2,400. When you get voltage that high, it'll do strange things."

Ed Hanauer nodded. "There's a short in the main feed somewhere, and someday it'll blow apart like a bomb going off."

With Hanauer, I could never be sure if he was lying or just pulling my leg, but I was certain of one thing: It was not a good thing to have 2,400 volts "leaking" underground.

"Sometimes when it's raining, it'll bite you pretty good," Rivers said, and with that, he and the other convicts began digging up a steam pipe that had begun to leak. I wasn't at all sure they ought to be digging there, but Hanauer was in charge and he said not to worry. Later, when Hanauer had to dig there with the backhoe, it was a different story, and then when the cable started sizzling . . .

But that was later, and I'm getting ahead of myself. We replaced the steam pipe without incident, the high-voltage line kept on leaking, and nobody seemed to think it a situation meriting concern.

Digging in the pen, no matter where, was always an adventure because there was no telling *what* we might hit. In the prison's 150 years of existence before I arrived, so much stuff had been built, pushed down, leveled off, and built on top of that nobody knew what lay where. Steam pipes, sewer drains, storm drains, gas lines, electric conduit, and water lines were everywhere. If we put a backhoe bucket in the ground, the question wasn't "Will we hit something?" but "Is it still being used?" Utilities might zigzag back and forth between buildings that no longer existed but still be connected at the far end to a less ancient building that was still in use.

Long about 1985, contractors were digging behind Housing Unit 3 to expand the exercise area for death row, and I began to hear rumors that workers had unearthed some old cells. I figured someone would stop me from getting too close, but I went on out and was delighted to find no one questioned me. I stepped over about eighteen inches of packed earth that still stood in front of the open doorway and into one of the cells. I looked around in awe. The walls were clean and appeared to have been painted white. Iron straps that had once served as hinges easily swung back at my touch, and the packed earth I had stepped over still showed the pattern of the wooden planks that had, at some time, been the door. It was apparent that the doors had been in good shape and were closed when the cells were buried sometime in the long

The buried cells behind Housing Unit 3 were uncovered in the mid-1980s. The cells, dating from circa 1848, were reburied after being photographed. Photo from the collection of Mark Schreiber.

forgotten past, and the dirt that had spent decades next to them had become like concrete, embracing the imprint of wood that had long since rotted away. I stretched out my arms and could put a palm on each side of the cell; I turned sideways and could almost reach end to end with my fingertips. In the very back of the cell was a small square hole up through the ceiling. Other than the door, that was the only opening in the small cramped space. I looked in each cell, as others there were also doing, with the hope of finding some small relic in the incredible time capsules, but the cells, determined to be circa 1848, were empty except for dirt. Once they'd been explored and photographed, the old cells were reburied, and with them all their untold stories. Those buried cells are still there today, waiting patiently behind Housing Unit 3 for someone to dig them back up and show them to the public.

Most of the time when maintenance had a backhoe project, Hanauer served as the operator. He loved to run the backhoe. He'd idle down the engine as slow as it would go and would then move the bucket as slowly and deliberately as he could. Every few minutes, he'd stop and tell the inmates, who would be leaning on shovels and picks, to climb down into the ditch and see what he had scraped or hooked with the bucket. Through it all, I would be perched on the backhoe's left fender and swapping stories with Hanauer.

In spite of Hanauer's mischievousness—some might say because of it—we had become pretty close. I'll admit that I admired his natural talent for kidding around with the inmates without pushing them too far (of course, it helped that he was just a grown-up kid—that is, if someone as short as Hanauer can be called "grown-up"). And I found he had some great stories about the prison to share, not just from his own illustrious career, but also from his dad's. Edward Hanauer Sr. had worked for the pen as a recreational officer in the late 1950s through the 1960s, so his son had been raised on stories about the staff and convicts who had populated the landscape of MSP during those violent times. In his youth, Hanauer Jr. had even played in prison ballgames and other sporting events that brought teams from the mid-Missouri area into MSP to play convict teams.

About half the time we had to get out the backhoe, it would be to dig up a broken water line, so the ditch would be full of water and mud. Sometimes it was a broken sewer pipe and the ditch was full of water and, well, other stuff. Sometimes it wasn't a broken water or sewer pipe until *after* Hanauer started digging. Probably the worst such mishap was when we were digging up a leaking steam line and Hanauer hit a sewer pipe. I can truthfully assert that stuff stinks even worse when it's boiled. Luckily, as he continued to try to clean out the ditch, he hit a storm drain, and suddenly the swirling, bubbling swill disappeared and a cheer went up from the

inmate plumbing crew. I believe they would have clapped for him if
they hadn't had one hand occupied holding their noses.

One time we were running new sewer lines along the wall
from Tower 4 to Tower 2, coming together at the back side of
the gym, and going across to Housing Unit 2. Hanauer would
dig about ten feet and then shut off the backhoe while I had the
inmates clean out the ditch. As they cleaned, Hanauer worked on
his lunch of cold chicken, disposing of the bones in the ditch. We
had been talking about the chances of digging up an unknown
graveyard (one had been rumored to be on the upper yard), and
each time he threw a bone, he hollered, "Hey! Isn't that a bone?
Look over there, just to your right. Isn't that a bone? I think we've
just found the graveyard." Then he would chuckle to me that one
of the tower officers was trying to see what he was talking about.

The next day the upper yard was closed and our job was
delayed. The chief engineer gave me a roll of caution tape and
some sharpened wooden slats and told me to put it all around the
area where we had dug. He explained to me that somebody had
informed the central office that we had found human bones and
they were sending someone to inspect the site. Until they gave
us permission to resume, that whole area was off limits to everybody. Hanauer kept telling me, and our convict helpers, not to tell
anybody that he had been yelling anything about bones. About a
week later, we were allowed to finish the job.

Years later, after Hanauer had been promoted to run
maintenance at Tipton Correctional Center, he came back for a
visit, and as we walked along the upper yard, Mark Schreiber, the
MSP relic who by then had become the associate superintendent,
joined us. As we talked and visited, I reminded Hanauer about
his chicken bone stunt, and Schreiber did not find it funny. It
turned out that he was the chief investigator at the central office
at the time, and he was the one who had halted our work while he
came out and looked for human remains.

Lest someone get the wrong idea about Schreiber's sense of

humor, I must say here that he was actually quite the prankster himself. When I was working in the engineer's office, he would drop in every morning to discuss the state of the institution and emergencies needing attention. About twice a week, he'd make up some calamity, such as, "Larry, the ice machine quit again this weekend, and it's supposed to get really hot today. How soon can you get on that?" When I wouldn't take him seriously, he'd not crack a smile, insisting there was a real emergency until he convinced me. Then he'd laugh and tell everyone how he'd gotten me. So when one Monday in 2002, Schreiber told me that part of the perimeter wall had fallen down over the weekend, I said, "Sure it did," and ignored him. I knew the inside of that section really had fallen out recently and had left the wall weakened, but Schreiber had already come in exclaiming that the rest of that section had tumbled down, and he wasn't going to get me twice with the same gag. Then someone else came in talking about the fallen wall. After that, Schreiber christened it the Larry E. Neal Memorial Wall. He said its falling down on the job reminded him of me. But back to Hanauer.

As eager as Hanauer normally was to run the backhoe, there came a job when he wanted no part of it. About a year after Rivers had shown me his shovel trick, the MSP administration decided to turn the vocational-technical building into a dorm. The bosses, who had been informed of the underground electric "leak," told Hanauer to dig the ditch for the steam to come into the vo-tech building. Hanauer turned white and found a dozen excuses to have someone else do it. When the response was he would do it or go home, he agreed, but only if I would help him.

I found out just how slow Hanauer could go on the backhoe. He would dig a little bit and have me climb down in the ditch and poke around with the shovel to see if I could locate the 2,400-volt cable. He kept telling me it was safe and not to worry, but all the while, I'm thinking, "If it could hurt him sitting on a rubber-tired tractor, then it isn't safe for me to be on the ground

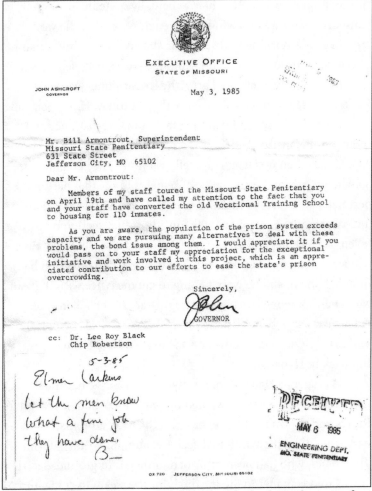

A note from Missouri Governor John Ashcroft after he took a tour of
MSP. It was during the conversion of the Vocational Training School
into dorms that Hanauer hit the 2,400-volt cable with the backhoe.

poking around with a shovel." I wouldn't have taken Hanauer's
word for my safety, but I didn't think the big shots would have
allowed us out there if it weren't safe. I've learned a lot since then.

Hanauer kept insisting that he knew the cable went through
that area and he could not miss hitting it, but finally he had

the ditch dug, all but a last scoop or so, and he relaxed. Then it happened. With a noise of frying and popping and sizzling, the line shorted out. Black smoke boiled out of the ground, and I, still standing next to the backhoe, looked to Hanauer, but he was gone! I eventually located him peeking around the far corner of the building. He began frantically waving at me and shouting, "Get away from there!"

All of maintenance was called to the scene. The power was killed, the line was exposed, and several people began taping it up with black tape. After it was determined that the affected section had been isolated, one of the electricians was sent to turn on the loop from the other direction, but somebody had miscalculated something. Floyd Frank, the assistant chief engineer, was sitting on the ground and had part of the wire on his lap. Suddenly he threw it down and yelled, "Get away from it! It's coming back on!"

Fire and smoke burst from the cable, knocking Donald Newby, the electrical foreman, away from the splice he was working on and blackening his arms up past his elbows. Brisk, an inmate electrician, shot up out of an electrical manhole that he had been working in. He went five feet up into the air, then over five feet, and then came down running. We all got back several feet and watched in awe as the cable burned to a crisp. After the power was again killed, Frank inspected the bare, burned wire and decided the only thing left to do was to call in contractors and have them pull new cable to get the power restored.

A few days later, I put my hand on the fence and the old tingle was gone. I don't mean I had less affection for the old fence; it just didn't move me as it had in the past. I made up my mind about one thing. The next time Hanauer asked me to get down in a ditch with a shovel, I'd take the shovel and hit him on the head with it. Then I'd bury him. The grounds of MSP might as well have one more useless relic buried on its grounds. "Who knows?" I thought. "Maybe the next guy digging there will call out, 'Hey, isn't that a bone down there?'"

Chapter 14

Leaving an Impression

One of the things I always liked about construction work was having something to show for my efforts. When a construction job is done, a worker can point to what he's made and say, "See that? I did that," and feel a sense of pride. I took a special pride in the job I did remodeling the inmates' dining room ramp. I sure left my mark with that job.

The dining room ramp had been added to the exterior of the food service building and then closed in so inmates could move from their dining room to the building's main corridor a level above without going outside. By about 1995, the old ramp had deteriorated to the point that it leaked when it rained and had several holes rusted through its walls. Louie Markway, who was at that time the maintenance supervisor over all of the M&M shops, believed the way to repair it was to buy some old building material from State Surplus Property and use it to cover the ramp. The material he chose was from an old military building and it consisted of two sheets of metal, one flat and one ribbed, with a layer of two-inch foam insulation between them. There was no taking the layers apart.

I tried to convince Markway that it wouldn't work for two reasons. First, the old ramp was so rusted that there was a good chance it wouldn't hold all of the extra weight, and second, the ribs on the roof would be running across the slope instead of up and down with it. I was afraid that would hold more water on the roof instead of letting it run off. I thought that Markway had asked my opinion because he knew that I had worked on several construction jobs and so wanted my advice. What he wanted, I soon realized, was for me to congratulate him for having such a good idea and to tell him how smart he was.

We used a skill saw to cut the material. Skill saws are made for cutting wood. To use them on metal requires turning the blades backwards to avoid shards and splinters. But then the blades don't cut so much as they split and slash the metal apart. Now if you have never cut metal in this way, you don't know what you've missed. The metal screams as the saw tears into it, and the longer the cut, the shriller the shriek becomes. That's with normal, single-sheet metal. Add a layer of foam for a low vibrating moan, and a second sheet of metal for a high-pitched howl, and the result is a racket something worse than the sound of ultimate suffering.

We had several people check on us while we sawed to be sure that nobody was being murdered, and it was rumored among the inmates that we were torturing people. I heard later that not a single violation was written for three days, nor did a single officer have an inmate smart off for a week. The noise was also heard out in town, and the police reported a drop in crime in the vicinity of the prison. I imagine criminals hunkered down in their hideouts, listening to the wailing screams coming from inside the prison walls, crossing themselves, and swearing off crime forever.

We put the material on the inside of the ramp for the walls and screwed it on from the outside. Then we put sections on top of the ramp and screwed them on from the inside. It looked good and certainly was a lot warmer than before. Markway was bragging about how well it had worked and reminding me how I had doubted him. But he got quiet when it began to rain. Every drop that hit the ramp found a way inside until the interior of the ramp took on the appearance of a doomed submarine. Floyd Frank was the assistant chief engineer at the time, so he came out and looked at it, and he decided that the outside needed to be covered with metal on the roof and sides.

All of this took place when I was working in the plumbing shop, and Richard Baumann complained that every time a special job came along, either me, Ed Hanauer, or both of us would get to go do something different. Meanwhile, he was forever stuck in the plumbing shop, struggling to keep the work orders caught up. It would be nice, he said, to get to do something besides plumbing once in a while.

Markway and Ralph Sanders, the maintenance supervisor who ran the carpenter shop, got together and ordered the material, and when it came in, Markway called me up to his office and told me that I would be helping Sanders finish the ramp. I started to tell him that I thought it would be a good idea if I stayed in the plumbing shop and Baumann went and helped on the ramp. Markway exploded into a verbal barrage of accusations: I was always arguing with him, I was always trying to get out of work, I never would do what he wanted me to do, I was always causing trouble, I always knew better than anyone else, and basically, I was personally responsible for every problem in the institution. I tried to explain that I wasn't trying to get out of work and I would do whatever he told me, but that I thought . . .—He interrupted me at that point and informed me that thinking wasn't my strong suit and that he was the boss and to quit arguing and do what I was told. Of course, this recollection is from my point of view; Markway would probably have a whole different perspective. He might share all the things I did to drive him crazy. Sometime, I need to tell the story about locking him in the M&M bathroom. And the time I superglued him to his chair—now that was really funny.

We got started putting the metal on in early December. The weather was nice, and it was the kind of job that I really enjoyed. Sanders was always fun to work with, and we had three hard-working inmates. In addition to adding the extra metal, we were adding a landing and door. We poured the concrete, built the addition, and got the metal on the roof before the weather got too bad. By the time we started on the sides, it was January and the temperature had dropped. We had mounted two-by-fours on the sides running lengthwise and had started mounting the metal vertically. The ramp was built with some arch in it (not for structural strength; someone just hadn't really known what he was doing), so each piece had to be cut at a different angle, and the angles at the top and the bottom weren't the same either. We had four sawhorses set up to hold the twenty-foot-long sheets of metal. I was cutting it to length as Sanders would get the measurements and the angle, then the inmates would install it by screwing it to the two-by-fours.

One morning as we were getting close to finishing the job, it was very cold, windy, and blowing snow, so I asked Markway if we could put the job off until better weather. His response was that we should have been done a week ago and we would stay on the job until it was finished.

He came out to look at the job about ten o'clock. After he left, Sanders called me aside and told me that Markway said it was too cold to be working, especially with the wind gusting, and he wanted Sanders to go back to M&M but I was to keep working out there because Markway wanted me to learn a lesson. Sanders told him that no one should be working in that weather, but if I had to stay out there, then he was going to stay, too. He said that had made Markway mad and he stomped off in a huff.

We stopped pretty often and would go in the back door of the staff dining room to warm up and get coffee and then get back to work. We put a full piece of metal—twenty feet long—on the sawhorses, and then Sanders went to help the inmates put up the last piece I had cut. I was bending over the metal to mark where it should be cut when the wind caught it. Suddenly I was flying. I was thrown about twenty feet and rolled upon landing. Stunned and confused, my face in the dirt, I could hear people yelling and running, but I was having a hard time understanding what had happened and where I was. When they turned me over, my eyes were full of blood and I could feel it running down my face. Then people were shouting and running again and all in all just carrying on something awful. They brought some water and paper napkins, and I washed some of the blood out of my eyes and off my face. Blood continued to pour from the bridge of my nose, and Sanders said it looked like it was cut at least an inch deep, eyeball to eyeball.

I was taken to an emergency room, where I expected to get stitches. When you get hurt like that, the number of stitches is very important. It gives you bragging rights. You can sit around with the guys and say, "Only twelve stitches? When I was cut across my nose they had to stitch the inside up with six stitches and then the outside took fourteen! Shoot! Twelve stitches ain't nothing." However, the doctor was concerned that stitches might cause it to scar worse. Of course, it's the same with scars: The worse the scar, the bigger the bragging rights. But I wound up with nothing but tape and assurances that the scar shouldn't be too bad, if there was a scar at all. I tried to take the news like a man, but I could see the day had gone from bad to worse.

When I got back to the institution, one staff member looked me up and congratulated me as if I had won the lottery.

"What do you mean, *congratulations*?" I asked.

"A scar on your face could win you thousands from the state," he responded, "especially when you'd been made to work outside in that kind of weather."

I shrugged. "I'm not suing the state. It isn't that big of a deal."

"But it is. A scar like that would hurt your looks, and that's worth a lot of money."

I laughed.

"I was born ugly and I'll die ugly, and a scar ain't going to make any difference."

He looked at me like I was crazy, and I could tell he wished it had been him that had gotten slammed in the face instead of me. Well, that made two of us.

Sanders took me around to the jobsite and showed me the dent my nose had put in the metal.

"How hard do you suppose your nose had to hit to crush the rib on that kind of sheet metal?" he wondered.

Later when we finished the job, I made sure that I put the piece with the dent where it could be seen on the ramp. And from time to time, I'd have the opportunity to point it out and say, "See that? My nose made that. Beat that with scars and stitches."

Chapter 15

Is There a Doctor in the House?

I spent more than two decades at MSP and never was attacked, hurt, or injured by an inmate. Well, at least not on purpose (that I know of). In one of my prison newsletter stories, I mentioned that I was a lot safer working at the pen than I had been when I worked in construction. When my wife read that, she began to remind me of the many emergency room trips I had made from MSP.

That windblown sheet of metal that sent me to the ER was not the first time the inmates' dining room ramp had been the scene of a mishap. Years earlier, on a morning cold enough to freeze snot, I was called from the staff dining room at about seven o'clock to fix a burst steam line. The problem was in a small steam heater that hung at the top of the ramp. At the top and bottom of the ramp were short landings, with the ramp itself running about sixty feet.

The staff dining room was on the same level of the building as the top of the ramp. I could hear the howling of the steam escaping the pipe as soon as I stepped out of the staff dining room and into the hall. A thick fog of steam was filling the area of the corridor near the ramp. With much caution, I entered the cloud. I was careful to avoid the scalding steam escaping the heater. As I eased across the landing, I had the sensation of sliding downward, but the fog was so thick I couldn't see, and I thought the sliding sensation was just some trick of the haze. I never considered that the ramp might be cold enough for the moisture to freeze into a sheet of ice. Then two things happened at once: I realized the noise of blowing steam was getting fainter, and I shot out of the fog.

I was about halfway down the ramp and still gaining speed. The inmates gathered at the bottom of the ramp to witness the blowing steam were shocked at my appearance and parted like the Red Sea. This gave me a good view of the hard wall awaiting me, but before I could consider how to soften our meeting, I came to the end of the ice. I was suddenly turning cartwheels, something I had always wanted to be able to do but had never been able to accomplish.

Before I could admire how well I was doing my new trick, the wall got in my way. I don't have a clear recollection of the next few minutes, but the inmates said that it was amazing how far back up the ramp I bounced. Nobody at the top knew I had taken off, and they were still waiting for me to exit the fog and tell them I could fix the heater. To tell you the truth I had forgotten all about the broken heater. Fortunately, though, I wasn't badly injured and avoided going to the hospital that time.

On another occasion, Ed Hanauer, some inmates, and I were unstopping a sewer line down in the industry area near the train gate. We had opened three manholes and had spent the morning trying to find and remove the blockage. Because we had a lot of tools out and didn't want to close everything up, we had asked to have some sandwiches brought to us. Most of the guys took the chance to relax against a four-foot retaining wall next to the furniture factory. I was up on the road above them, and every time my sandwich dripped some ketchup, I managed to be above Gritter.

Each time the ketchup splattered on his neck or back, he would warn me he was going to have to hurt me. Each time he warned me, I squeezed my sandwich a little tighter. I felt secure knowing he'd have to climb the wall to get to me. When a big drop landed on his ear, Gritter turned to Hanauer and said, "Ed, I'm gonna have to kill him." To which Hanauer replied, "I don't know why you've put up with it this long." (This from a guy who made a career out of tormenting inmates.) Gritter made a quick

turn and grab for me, but laughing at him, I took a couple of
quick steps backward.

I had forgotten all about the open manhole behind me.

I didn't know what was happening except I was getting
a whole lot shorter in a hurry. My armpits stopped me from
completely disappearing into the manhole and becoming another
plug in the sewer system. I had stepped into the manhole with
only one foot; the other was in front of my face. I was stuck and
expected Gritter to finish his sandwich over my head when I
heard the tower officer shout down to me, "Should I shoot him?
Is he attacking?" I couldn't see the officer from my position, but
the others told me that he actually ran out onto the catwalk with
his shotgun, believing that I had been attacked. But Gritter wasn't
attacking; he was laughing, and so was everybody else. I really
believe I have brought more joy to people by getting hurt than by
any other method.

The part of me that was in the manhole was dangling about
ten feet above the bottom. With no footholds available, I couldn't
get my arms in a position to push myself up, so I had to endure
the whole plumbing crew gathering around me, commenting on
my predicament, asking stupid questions, and laughing at my
feeble attempts to extricate myself. Finally it was time to go back
to work and they needed me out of the way to access the sewer,
so they pulled me out. I had a pretty bad scrape the length of my
back but again avoided going to the emergency room. I wasn't so
lucky in the boiler room mishap.

That time, I was working in the basement of the hospital
building with a tall inmate with a crippled leg named Slim (the
inmate was named Slim, not his leg; this isn't *Mary Poppins*).
Slim was a hard worker, but he had a few empty cells in his
block. He had been on death row for a while and now that he
was out, he was constantly worried that he would get accused
of something he didn't do—what the inmates called getting a
"free case"—and would be sent back to the row. Slim and I were

replacing a broken pipe in the boiler room, and I had squatted down to look under some pipes. I raised myself up directly under a broken valve handle and hit it so hard I was nearly knocked out. The blow sent me down to my knees.

Slim had seen what had happened and came to help me up. I was trying to stand, wondering what had happened to me, when Slim said, "You're bleeding!" and indeed I was. I had cut a deep notch in the top of my head, and blood was pouring down into my eyes and down the back of my head onto my shirt. I couldn't walk too well, so Slim had to help me up the stairs to the dental clinic area where Charlie Gann was the officer on duty.

Slim greeted Gann with, "I didn't do it! He did it to himself! I didn't hit him. I didn't have nothing to do with it!" He was certain that I was mortally wounded, and he would be charged with my murder. Gann helped Slim get me on the elevator and called the engineering office to let them know I would need to go to the ER. Slim helped me stagger down to the control center, proclaiming his innocence to every person we met. At the control center we were met by Chief Engineer Elmer Larkins and Assistant Engineer Floyd Frank, but before I left with them I turned to Slim and said, "Why did you hit me? I didn't do anything to you." He never again went on a job where he would be alone with me.

Another time I was inspecting some welding being done in 5-C, and as I turned the corner, someone in the machine shop began to grind on a weld and the dust hit me in the face. I knew I had gotten some of it in my eyes and I flushed them as best I could, but my right eye continued to feel irritated. A couple of days later, it seemed to clear up, but about a week after that, I noticed I was having trouble seeing out of that eye. In a few more days, it was almost blind.

Again I went to the emergency room, and the folks there sent me to an eye doctor who explained that I had a small piece of metal in the center of my pupil. It had healed over, but then the sliver began to rust, with the rust spreading over the pupil.

The doctor informed me that he would have to freeze my eye and grind on it until he had removed the metal and rust. He said I wouldn't feel it as he did it, but for the next few days, it might be painful. He asked me if I had ever suffered from welder's burn, and when I told him I had, he said this would be much worse. That was not at all what I wanted to hear, but it turned out to be the truth.

Other mishaps ending in ER visits were when I broke a finger while moving some one-inch square tubing out of the bus shed and when a large rubber band snapped and struck my right eye. But the story that Hanauer always wanted me to tell took place in the area between the receiving building and the hospital.

We had dug up a large section of the pavement to run a steam line from the hospital into the receiving building and had placed a sheet of plywood across the ditch, which was about four feet wide and five feet deep. We had lunch delivered and during the break someone (not me this time) began throwing little chunks of mud at someone else. In a few minutes everyone was tossing pieces of mud at one another, and each time the clumps got a little bigger. Then an inmate called Biggin, who was good help, picked up a clump almost too large for one hand and took aim at an inmate near me. Distracted with eating, I saw Biggin had missed his aim, and the clump was instead coming toward me. I put up a hand to ward it off, but the clump was far heavier than I expected, being comprised more of rock than dirt. It brushed my fingers aside and hit me on the head with a thud.

I slumped beneath the unexpected blow but then tried to recover without appearing hurt. We all glanced toward the nearest tower officer. Would he report the incident as an attack by an inmate on staff? To our relief, we found him intently looking out into the street.

Everyone's attention then redirected to me, and expressions shifted back from relief to alarm.

"You're bleeding!" Hanauer announced.

He was right. Once again, I was pumping blood out of the top of my head. Hanauer examined the gash and declared it would require stitches.

"No, I'll be all right," I said. I was certain it had been an accident and didn't want to get anyone in trouble, including me, as I had thrown some of the mud myself. Finally Biggin looked at it and agreed I had best go to the doctor to have my head examined (not the first time that had been suggested). I agreed, as the blood continued to flow freely, but I had a plan to keep from getting anyone in trouble without having to lie about what happened. I waited until an officer came out of the control center gate and walked toward him, turning to say something to Hanauer just as I reached the ditch for the steam line. I deliberately missed the plywood and "fell" into the ditch. As the officer and Hanauer came running up, I raised up out of the ditch, clapped a hand to my head and began to moan, "Oh, my head; oh, my head."

The officer radioed for help, and then he explained what he had witnessed to those who came to assist me. Nobody ever asked for my version. I was just taken to the emergency room, where the doctor said, "You again!?"

Chapter 16

To the Max: The Prison inside the Prison

Sometime around 1988, I was assigned to work in the Special Management Facility, or SMF, the behavior modification and administrative segregation unit of MSP. This was where all of the most dangerous inmates were kept. The area consisted of Housing Unit 5, with 5-A and 5-B, and Housing Unit 5-C, also called Supermax. SMF was a prison inside the prison, complete with its own superintendent and major.

An inmate's first stop in SMF was Supermax, where he remained in a bare cell 24/7 except for exercise. After several months of good behavior in Supermax, he could go to 5-A, where he was allowed a few more privileges, such as recreation and eating in the Supermax dining room. He would still not be allowed to have electrical appliances in his cell. After successfully completing that stage (which often included several more extended visits to Supermax), the inmate would be on a sort of probationary period until he was allowed to go back out to the general population.

My first visit to SMF, outside of the tour I got in training, came when I was a labor foreman. I was delivering ten gallons of gas to maintenance supervisor David Finnigan for some welding behind Supermax. The building was only about a year old at the time, and I wondered why it would need extensive welding repair so soon after opening. I didn't have to wonder very long because everyone was ready to tell me about the building's diverse problems. It seemed everyone was laughing at the "idiots" who designed and built it, but it wasn't happy laughing; it was sneering at the waste of taxpayer money on an unusable building.

Expensive high-security light fixtures had been installed; it took the inmates all of one day to dismantle them, turn the parts into shanks, then hide the shanks inside the "restored" fixture itself. The inmates also kicked open some doors, and one small guy broke the unbreakable glass in the window and crawled out. The body-building inmate who had sneered at my training class could not be contained when he became a 5-C resident, and I learned that Finnigan needed the gas I was delivering so he could weld sheets of one-quarter-inch steel inside the cell to make it muscleman-proof. Forever after, that cell was known simply as "the steel cell." Contractors had replaced the doors, maintenance had replaced the four-foot fluorescent fixtures with porcelain pull-chain fixtures, the windows had been modified by welding a piece of square tubing vertically in the center of them, and so many other flaws were fixed that I can't remember them all. Everyone had something bad to say about the building.

When he assigned me to SMF, Bill Wieberg, who had been my supervisor since I came to work at the pen, explained that I was not being punished nor was I being moved because he had found me lacking in ability or devotion to duty. It was just that Tom Walsh, the maintenance supervisor over SMF, had convinced the chief engineer that he had to have more help—preferably someone actually capable of doing repair work—and so I was being moved.

I asked Ed Hanauer what that speech was all about, and he said that ever since Supermax had opened, the bosses had sent all of the worthless help over there and he wasn't at all surprised that I was being condemned to that wasteland of useless employees. I told him Wieberg had carefully explained that he thought of me as good help. Hanauer smirked and said Wieberg would say that, but I shouldn't take it too seriously.

"He was told to send someone, and you were the one he felt he could get along without," Hanauer concluded.

With a sinking heart, I picked up my few belongings, said my goodbyes to the plumbing shop, and made my way to what seemed like the end of the world. At M&M, anyone might come walking in, but in SMF we were out of sight, out of mind. My new supervisor, Walsh, was a little less than two years from retirement. He had a high, quivery, nasal voice that made him sound like his feelings had just gotten hurt. He was more concerned about keeping the shop clean and the floor waxed than anything else. Many times we would have to stop a repair job and sit on the steps in the hall while we waited for the floor to dry.

You know, obsessive-compulsive people are easy to mess with. Everything had to be clean, in its place, and just like Walsh wanted before he left at the end of the day. Walsh insisted that the shop's three-way light switches be managed so that when he left, he could flip the switch down to turn the lights off. Sometimes when he was out of the shop, I would turn the lights out at the door and back on at the elevator. Then when he would lock up at night, he would try to flip off the lights and find the switch was backwards. After whining that somebody had gotten the lights all messed up, he would turn the lights off at the door, grumble all the way to the back of the shop and turn them on with that switch, and then go back to the door to turn them off in the down position.

And Walsh was just one of the interesting SMF characters. Bill Miller, a small but wiry, white-haired old gentleman, loved to joke around, but was also extremely capable and had a great knowledge of the air conditioning field. I had already gotten to know him at M&M, where he had worked in the refrigeration shop. He took care of the ice machine and the heating, ventilation, and air conditioning systems. Lester Martin was the electrician who had worked at MSP for years. He was the opposite of Miller in every way, heavy and with a sour disposition. He was nearing retirement and was determined to live long enough to see it, but he was battling major health problems. He would leave 5-C about three p.m. in order to be at the front door by four p.m.

It took him so long because there were several flights of stairs between Supermax and the prison's main corridor. He would labor up one flight, then stop and lean on the railing, gasping for breath. Then, after smoking a cigarette, he would give a groan and a sigh, and tackle the next set of steps. The first few times I saw him struggling along, I thought he needed to be taken to the hospital. At no time would I have been surprised if he suddenly collapsed and died.

Martin had a desk up in the penthouse and kept the electrical tools up there. He literally spent the day smoking cigarettes and reading. When an electrical issue came up, he would send one or both of the two inmates assigned to him, with the tools and parts needed to do the repair work. If they ran into a problem, they would call him for advice. When he absolutely had to go to the area that needed repair, he would, but at his own speed and complaining all the way. Martin did make it to retirement, but he didn't survive long after that.

The other member of our crew was Ted Clutter, who would collect a toolbox full of plumbing tools and a bucket of parts and disappear into the tunnels of Housing Units 5-A and 5-B with his two inmates. They would emerge for lunch and then vanish again, coming back to the shop just in time to go home. He kept all the plumbing done; how busy he stayed, I don't really know. I would not have noticed when he retired except that his inmate workers were around a lot more.

When I got to 5-C, I was shown what I needed to do to keep the plumbing working and began to learn to work on the kitchen equipment. That was always fun. Walsh and Miller would go together to work on it, and I would tag along and watch. They would argue and call each other names and get mad about how to fix the problem. Miller would usually get his way and do the repair work. All the time Walsh would be fussing and whining that Miller was going to tear everything up. And when the work was done, he would take credit when it worked and blame Miller when it didn't.

With the inmates in SMF, we had a hard time controlling the manufacture of hooch, the homebrewed alcohol. Inmates addicted to booze were the ones most commonly in trouble, and SMF was the area set aside for punishment. Many of the SMF residents were on a continual circuit; they would make it back to the general population, then get drunk and return to SMF to be locked up again. We hired our guys from this pool, and they most certainly had not been rehabilitated. They hadn't even considered it.

Concealing the manufacture and distribution of hooch was a time-honored tradition of the occupants of MSP; finding and destroying it was a high priority for the staff. Both sides had learned from previous generations, but the inmates had several advantages. While both the inmates and the staff knew the unsuccessful hiding places, only the inmates knew where and when we had failed to discover the hooch. For another thing, the prison was the inmates' whole life, while it was only our job. They had more time to think, watch, and study—and they were powerfully motivated to succeed.

Almost any food or semi-food product that would rot could be turned into alcohol, and many inmates were desperate enough to drink alcohol in any form. Consequently, the canteen did not sell either mouthwash or hair tonic containing alcohol. The most common stock used to make homebrew was either potatoes or fruit, and anywhere with a source of heat could be used to cook it off. The warmer, the better. The penthouse, filled with steam lines for the heating units, was a bootlegger's gold mine, and Walsh and Miller would make a raid there nearly every week. They would pour out the booze, but neither of them wanted to write anyone up. Even when one of the workers was found under the influence, the worst they would do was send him back to his cell to sleep it off.

Over at M&M, Hanauer had made it clear that if hooch was found in any of the plumbing shop areas, the whole crew would be fired. This gave inmates an excuse for telling a wayward guy they were not going to let him put their jobs in jeopardy by cooking off a batch. If threats failed, an inmate would let us know that it might be best if this guy wasn't in the shop. They wouldn't snitch him out and say why, just drop a word of advice that this guy didn't belong. This would normally come from one of the older guys who had been with us for a while. Walsh felt that over in SMF that method wouldn't work because most of the guys available to hire had already proven they were going to make hooch at some time. Other than that, they were very good workers, some of them having spent several years working at M&M.

Walsh was right. At M&M we might keep workers several years and get them up to top pay, so they had high incentives to keep their job. In SMF, they wouldn't work longer than six months, and most wouldn't last that long without a write-up. If we were going to use inmates—and we were expected to give them jobs as part of their probationary recovery incentive—then we had to choose from people who were willing to risk being returned to 5-C just to get that long-anticipated drink. And if we wrote them up and fired the crew every time we found their booze, we would always be training a new crew, and there just weren't all that many capable guys in 5-B.

Finally Walsh started a rumor that we didn't always pour out the hooch, but that when we found some that had been hidden really well, he would urinate in it. The inmates really didn't believe him, but I guess homebrew always has a funny taste and they could never be sure. (Knowing Walsh I wasn't too sure myself.) I don't know that this even slowed them down and it sure didn't stop them, although they often complained that they couldn't really enjoy the hooch anymore. Walsh would squeak, "Well, I know there was some that you sure couldn't have enjoyed." Then he'd add, "But you wouldn't drink it if it tasted bad, would you? No, I'm sure you didn't drink that!"

——|—|—|——

The shop was under the kitchen in the middle of the Supermax building, and the ceiling was nearly hidden with conduit, water pipes, steam lines, waste drainpipes, and ductwork. One time a floor drain in the kitchen stopped up and all efforts to unplug it failed. Miller mentioned that all the drain lines in our area had hubless connectors and could easily be taken apart and cleaned from below. An almost panic-stricken Walsh, thinking of the mess we might create, said that we couldn't even try that as the nasty, sludgy, rotten-smelling wastewater would spray all over the place. Miller didn't think it would be that bad. The drain emptied into the main drain line back by the elevator. This was as far from Walsh's desk as it could be, and Miller thought we could take it apart back there with a barrel under it and run a snake back towards the drain and keep most of it off the floor.

Walsh wasn't convinced. He said the shop would stink and the nasty stuff in the trap was bound to get on everything. He forbade us to try until it became apparent, even to him, that it was the only way. At that time we had one big, round inmate who was known to everybody as Bulldog. He cautiously took apart the pipes. Nothing came out. We ran a snake up one pipe and stirred up quite a stink and did get a little black kitchen waste on the floor. Walsh was running around cleaning it up and whining about the mess and especially the horrible, putrid smell. The closest I'd ever come to smelling something like it was the time my brother hid a half-rotten skunk under the backseat of my 1959 Ford Galaxy 500. The waste smell was even worse.

When we failed to get it unstopped, we went to the next joint and took it apart, while Walsh increased the volume of his whining and complaining. As we got closer to Walsh's desk, there was more black, rotten garbage, and the pungent aroma began bringing tears to our eyes. We could not get to any more fittings, except the one fastened to the trap itself, and that was almost over Walsh's desk. Holding a handkerchief over his nose, Walsh absolutely forbade us from taking that one apart. After we had spent

over an hour and had made no progress, Miller said we would
have to loosen it from the trap. Walsh couldn't stand to watch, so
he left, warning us to have it all cleaned up before he returned.
I told Bulldog to be very careful not to get a bunch in his face. I
told him how to put up plastic sheeting and warned him when
it came out it would flood all over him. I had already told him
this about the other two joints that didn't flood, and he no longer
believed me.

The trap was very hard for Bulldog to reach, as he had to go
over several pipes to get to it. He grunted and cursed and worked
at it, pushing the plastic out of his way, tugging and twisting for
quite a while. All the time I kept advising him to keep his mouth
shut. He was getting angry, jerking on the joint and muttering,
when suddenly the joint came loose and the black, oily mal-
odorous garbage gushed out. It mostly missed me because I was
behind him and he was rather large, but it splashed off pipes, ceiling, and ductwork, spewing a foul horrible atrocious mess over
everything, including not only Walsh's desk but also his chair.

Shocked into immobility, Bulldog froze where he was, covered head to foot, his face a ghastly black mask of dripping thick,
hideous goo. After several slow seconds had passed, he opened
his eyes, and Miller burst into a howling fit of laughter, gasping
that all he could see of Bulldog's face was his eyeballs peering out
of a black gumbo mask. The office was an appalling mess and
stank even worse than it looked. Black stuff was dripping to the
floor in little putrid globs. Bulldog was still too traumatized to do
anything but blink at us.

Finally I took him up to the hall and got him a shower
while the rest of the crew started cleaning up the horrific mess.
I didn't hurry back. It took weeks to get the office to the point
where the smell didn't assault whoever walked in, and poor old
Walsh never did get over it. I think in his mind we had taken his
little sanitary refuge from the world and turned it into a septic
tank. After that, each time he would lock up the shop in the eve-

ning, he would stop at the door, and with his shoulders stooped and his hand on the light switch, he would look back at the shop, sigh, shake his head mournfully, and close the door. I felt so bad for him that I even quit messing with the light switches. Well, at least for a little while.

Chapter 17

Ingenious Inmates

When people want an example of great human ingenuity, the feat that most often comes to mind is NASA putting a man on the moon. If I want an example of boundless resourcefulness, I look to the old breed of MSP convicts. These men embodied the motto, "We have done so much for so long with so little that we can now do anything with nothing."

One of the first examples of cleverness to amaze me was the homemade water heaters that every inmate and several of the square men possessed. The heaters consisted of two pieces of metal—most often stainless steel so they wouldn't rust—each about one inch by two inches. Separating the metal were various kinds of insulating material, from rubber gaskets to blocks of wood, and holding this sandwich together was some string or a rubber band.

Using a discarded electrical cord, like what might come off a lamp, the inmates would create a complete electrical circuit by attaching one wire from inside the cord to one metal side, and the cord's second wire to the second metal side. Dropped into a cup of coffee and plugged in, these heaters, called stingers, would have the drink boiling in just a few minutes. Although these contraptions were technically contraband, no one on the staff ever seemed concerned about them. Still being new to the prison environment when I first saw them, I was fascinated both by the stingers themselves and the staff's acceptance of them. In fact, I was to discover later on that the M&M shops were the main manufacturers of these inexpensive devices.

Anything that could be used to cook food was a valuable item to own or control inside the prison. The supply of black-market food items, most stolen from food services, never equaled the demand, despite the resourcefulness of the thieves and the lackadaisical attitude of many staff. While ready-to-eat foods were highly sought after for snacking, the foods that brought in the highest prices were those that required some preparation, especially protein dishes such as chicken, steak, eggs, and ham. The food market was an opportunity for the creative convict to profit.

Manufacturing a cooktop could be as simple as placing a high-watt lightbulb under an overturned one-gallon tin can. Of course, this required that someone procure, and convey into the cell block, the can, the bulb (150 or 200 watt, if possible), the bulb's porcelain fixture (optional but handy for holding the bulb in place), and the wires for connecting the bulb to the wall outlet. None of these items were by any means overly difficult for an inmate to come by. Requiring a little more thought and effort were the prison cell stoves. A basic but functional version took heating coils removed from either a coffee pot or perhaps a piece of kitchen equipment being worked on, or junked, in M&M. The coils would then be mounted to a can. These would get hotter than the lightbulb versions.

Inmates would also build stoves from scratch with a burner made from heating element wires taken from a toaster, electric space heater, or maintenance supply, or even brought in by a staff member. Usually these stoves were designed to blend into the cell surroundings, perhaps appearing to be a wooden footstool or a soda cooler, and thus would escape detection until a full-fledged shakedown would remove all of the contraband items from a housing unit. Those who could find nothing better would cook food on the fins of horizontally mounted steam heaters, uninsulated steam pipes, and even in the windowsills on the south side of Housing Unit 4, better known as A-Hall. On his luckiest day, an enterprising and especially likeable inmate might even talk the hall officer into letting him cook his food in the housing unit office's microwave oven.

Inmates had gardens everywhere. Tomato plants, pepper plants, melons, cucumbers, and other garden items were grown in little plots, in buckets, in cardboard boxes in windows, in anything and anywhere they could be coaxed to grow. The produce was usually picked long before it was ripe and allowed to ripen in an inmate's cell as inmates never trusted the other inmates or staff to leave it alone long enough for it to get ripe on the vine. These gardens were a constant source of trouble as many of the inmates used them as a place to hide their contraband. Knives were hidden in the dirt under the plants and were handy to get to and to put back. Often carefully trimmed marijuana plants grew in the middle of other plants, and one time a group of inmates made wine inside a growing watermelon.

The watermelon trick was done in the industries area, and the officer in that area knew the inmates were getting some homebrew from somewhere but couldn't figure out just where. He had searched the garden area a couple of times, suspecting there was a five-gallon bucket buried just under the surface; that had been done more than once. But this time, the inmates had cut a hole into the watermelon, inserted the starter ingredients, and let it cook right on the vine. They would unplug it while "tending" to the garden and drink the wine with a straw, then start another batch. Then they would seal up the plug with wax again, all right under the guard's nose. Finally the watermelon couldn't take it anymore and split open, sagged down, and released an aromatic clue that led the officer's nose right to the suddenly defunct still. The officer was the one to tell me the story and seemed to be proud of the ingenuity of his workers.

Hunger and thirst, however, weren't all that motivated convict invention. One time when I was walking down the walk in Housing Unit 2, I stopped in amazement at a cell filled with open electronics equipment. After a few moments I realized that the inmate (who totally ignored me) was watching a television that had been built from the insides of two different sets. The original sets were different name brands and originated in different decades. One had the receiver-tuner, sound, and video pre-amp, and then from there, wires carried the AC power and the video signal to the second TV that had a good high-voltage unit and picture tube.

Throughout most of the prison, inmates only watched whatever TV stations they could pick up from the airwaves without rabbit ears or antennas, as these were considered shank material and were removed before TVs and radios left the canteen. Convicts responded to the inconvenience with homemade antennas. Transformers from broken TVs and radios, as well as new ones swiped from the electricians' storeroom, were salvaged, and the long wires carefully unstrung. One end would be weighted and thrown as high out a window as possible and the other fastened to the antenna stub on the appliance. The cobweb of wires leading from walks to windows and then hanging on each building's exterior was one of the strange but accepted sights in MSP housing units.

Mirrors also helped the convicts watch TV. Sometimes an inmate without a TV would hold a mirror out of his cell to watch his neighbor's set. This might require some rearranging of the belongings of the neighbor, and, of course the TV's owner would have to turn up the volume.

That was just one use for mirrors; the inmates also used them to monitor their surroundings. Most cell blocks were laid out along the same lines. Cells were lined up in a row with a walkway in front of them. On the bottom level, or flag, the walkway was usually an open area several feet wide, but on the upper walks, the walkway was about three feet wide with a three-pipe railing. The front of the cell was usually all bars, with a door of bars in the middle. To get on the upper walks, I would have to have an officer unlock a gate, and the noise of the gate would draw the inmates' attention. A low murmur would float down the walk from cell to cell, and mirrors would pop out of the bars at an angle for the bearers to see who was in their area.

The first few times I saw this happen, I found it most unnerving to have all these disembodied eyes jumping out to look at me. Depending on the inmates' level of confinement, the mirrors might disappear as quickly as they had appeared when inmates realized with one quick glance that the visitor was only a square man. On punitive lockdown units, the mirrors and the eyes continued to float just outside the cells, following me all the way down the walk. Inmates in these cells milked every last ounce of diversion from the rare interruptions to come to their desolate impassive environment.

In Housing Units 2, 5-A, and 5-B, mirrors also enhanced visiting. Those housing units had beds mounted back to back on one-quarter-inch steel-plate walls, and convicts lying on their beds and visiting would often have a mirror out to see each other's faces. The convicts would even use strips of rags to tie checkerboards up between their cells so they could play checkers, card games, and dominoes with one another.

The inmates also showed inventiveness in their jobs. Perhaps the most infamous example was when an inmate named Roanie, Warden Donald Wyrick's pet snitch, was contracted to pour concrete bases for new toilets in A-Hall. As I understand it, Roanie was given several gallons of peanut butter for doing the job. The concrete was poured around the base of the old "flower pot" stool—so named because that's what the toilet resembled—and a new porcelain stool was mounted on top. This put the toilet about twelve inches off the floor and gave new meaning to the term "throne." The bottom floor of the housing unit went well enough for Roanie, but when he had to start packing cement up the stairs, he needed a shortcut. Suddenly he was using about half as much concrete, and at the same time, the housing unit started using twice as much toilet paper.

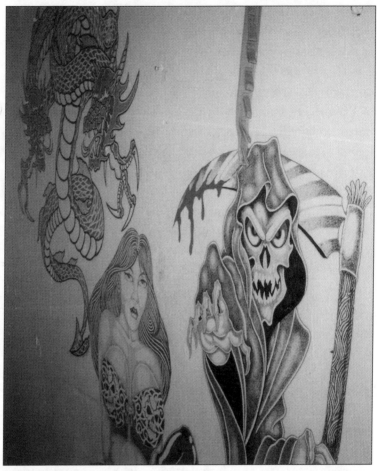

It was common for inmates to draw or paint on their cell walls. This particular artwork was in Housing Unit 3.

It was considered a joke, and nobody really believed he had used toilet paper as filler, but in the mid-nineties we knocked out some of those concrete pedestals, and sure enough, they were more than half toilet paper. At the time of our discovery, the state was getting tight with its toilet paper, and our inmates rejoiced at this unexpected supply. But their rejoicing soon ended. Apparently the paper was quite durable but terribly abrasive.

Inmate resourcefulness reached the highest levels in Housing Unit 5-C, Supermax, because the inmates in this most restrictive environment had to make each resource count. Their belongings were restricted to a mattress, sheets, blanket, pillow, and white jumpsuit.

The Supermax cell doors were solid except for a small glass window about twelve inches high and five inches wide. This meant the residents could not hand items from cell to cell as was possible in the housing units where the cells had all bar fronts. But it did not mean the Supermax inmates couldn't pass items back and forth. The tool for this job was a "cadillac," a simple string in non-prison parlance. The string would be thrown under one cell door to under another, and by adjusting the angle thrown and the length of string used, a cadillac could be made to go almost anywhere the sender wanted it to go. Once the cadillac was in the target cell, the giving inmate could tie on the item, and then the receiving inmate could pull it in. The items moved might be something small, like a cigarette, or something as big as a paperback book that a kind-hearted officer had given to a well-behaving inmate.

One opportunity for inmates in Supermax to get their hands on contraband came in the exercise yards. These yards were about three feet wide and twelve feet long, and the tops were made of chain-link fence. As two of the four Supermax exercise yards were located within throwing distance of the road, and as the road was higher than the yards, it was a simple matter to toss items through the chain link ceiling. The contraband was usually tobacco and paper, but could also be cigarettes, dope, food, or just something to help pass the tedious hours. Somehow the 5-C inmates managed to retrieve the items that got stuck even though the ceiling was about twelve feet off the ground. The items could then be shared, traded, or sold and were moved about the different cells with cadillacs.

Even when the chain link fencing was covered with rat wire and sheet metal, the inmates still managed to secure contraband from deliveries thrown on top. I never discovered how.

Shortly after Supermax opened, the inmate-proof fluorescent light fixtures were removed because the inmates were taking them apart. Porcelain light fixtures replaced the originals, and above these fixtures, in the poured concrete ceilings of the cells, were small metal boxes that held the wires for the lights. A conduit run connected the wire box in one cell to the wire box in the next. A convict with enough electrical savvy to understand the workings of electrical circuits, locked in his cell with nothing else to do, could find some diversion with the light fixtures. Removing the porcelain light fixture would gain him access to the wires in the small metal box. He could then cut one five-inch piece from the neutral wire and use it to connect the light fixture to the metal conduit box. The metal conduit then pulled double duty as the neutral and ground, and the lights were back on.

The remaining twelve feet of the neutral wire, which ran into the wire box in the next cell, could be pulled out after the inmate in the next cell disconnected his end. This long piece of wire could be used for weapons, cadillacs, and extension cords. The inmates did all of this without tools and without turning the electricity off in the circuits, which meant risking a shock of 110 volts—enough to make the inmate jump but not kill him, unless he fell into the toilet he was standing on to reach the light. Eventually, nearly half of the cells had this alteration, as this trade secret was passed from generation to generation of 5-C inmates.

When Supermax opened, inmates were allowed to have store-bought stingers—water heaters that were neither as quick nor as durable as the homemade ones—and their cells had an electrical outlet. I heard of an inmate who fastened the hot wire of a stinger cord to one end of a common pencil sharpened on both ends. Then, by touching the other end to a piece of metal, he could strike an arc and use the pencil as a makeshift cutting torch. With this tool, he cut a piece of metal from his toilet, which he sharpened by scraping it on the concrete floor. And he had himself a shank.

The Supermax inmates also learned that common dental floss could cut stainless steel metal. I found several stainless steel push buttons used to turn on the sink water that had been cut clean off. Cutting with dental floss just required patience, and the Supermax inmates had hour upon uninterrupted hour to pull the floss up and down over the top or from underneath the button. The floss produced a cut that was as slick as a factory finish.

What interested the inmates weren't the buttons themselves but the rods, about a quarter-inch round and a foot long, that rested behind the buttons. Once removed, these rods would be sharpened and then put back in place, and the button glued back on with toothpaste. (Toothpaste, I discovered, was used for a multitude of purposes and could hardly be refused to an inmate.) When the shank was needed, the button would be knocked off and the rod removed and used. If time permitted, it could even be returned to its hiding place. There was a plumbing closet between each pair of cells and anytime I was in one I would tap the ends of the rods with a hammer and occasionally was rewarded with hearing the sharpened rod fly into the cell. Officers would then remove the convict in handcuffs and retrieve the shank.

One day I was informed that I was to participate in an all-night shakedown. It started at Supermax. I was astounded by the amount of contraband the convicts had been able to accumulate in the bare unfurnished cells. It was that night that I saw the invention that amazed me more than anything else in all the years that I worked at MSP.

It was a superior class of cadillac, consisting of four mice in tandem harness. Each mouse had a collar of No.12 insulated wire (no doubt from our ceiling lights), with a thread harness tied on either side of this collar, from the lead mouse to the last, and then fastened to a small piece of wood behind them. The center of this wood had been attached to a long thread. The convicts had trained the mice to come to be fed when they heard the sound of scratching, and could send this little mouse team all over the wing; the thread they pulled behind them could then be used like the other cadillacs to move objects.

This little circus act was one more piece of MSP proof that even the most restrictive environment cannot put bars on the human imagination.

Chapter 18

The Great Flood in A-Hall

I knew I was in trouble when the water line broke in Cuddle Bear's cell.

Cuddle Bear was a burly weight-lifting convict, and other than his nickname, there was nothing sweet about him. He had been keeping a close watch on me the whole time I worked on his leaking toilet in A-Hall. He was not at all pleased when the one-inch pipe to the toilet broke right in two at the threads and water began surging onto the floor. It wasn't so much that he didn't like wet feet. He was concerned about all of his property.

The interior of A-Hall during the 1980s is one of those facts of the institution's past that no one now would imagine, or perhaps even believe, if there weren't photos. Also called Housing Unit 4, A-Hall was built circa 1865 by convicts, and during the time I worked at MSP it was the most desired living quarters in the whole institution. Only a few square feet short of the federally mandated cell size for three inmates, each cell had tons of room, relatively speaking, for two people. It was also a housing unit with high levels of inmate freedom, as the inmates who lived there were locked in their cells only at night. Assignment to one of A-Hall's coveted cells depended on two things: One, an inmate had to be on good terms with the warden, which often meant the inmate was a snitch, and two, he had to pay off the inmate who clerked for the movement officer. The clerk didn't have final say on cell assignments, exactly, but his advice on who could or couldn't handle the freedom of A-Hall was a powerful determining factor for the officer's assignment decisions.

The pool tables inside A-Hall (also called Housing Unit 4) in 1986.
A-Hall opened in 1868, making it the oldest building inside MSP during
Neal's career.

Not only did A-Hall offer extra space and freedom, but
the cells also had lots of natural light. Most housing units had
cell blocks in the building's center, but the four tiers of cells in
A-Hall were on the building's perimeter and there was an outside
window in every cell. In front of the A-Hall cells was a three-foot-
wide concrete walk that had a pipe railing; on the other side of
the railing was an open space to the cells on the building's other
side, with an occasional narrow bridge from one side to the other.
The steps were in the front corners of the building. Everything
was made of cut limestone, inside and out, except for the cell
floors, which were twelve-by-twelve weathered red brick tile,
and the bottom floor, or flag, which was made of poured concrete. The walls were plaster over large cut building stones. In the
1980s, paint of every color came into the housing unit at a rate of
ten or fifteen gallons a week. Many of the residents worked in the

furniture factory, where they would build elaborate furniture for the cells, then disassemble it and pack it piece by piece into the housing unit where they would put it back together. During that all-night shakedown I mentioned, all contraband, including the wooden furniture, was broken up and hauled out. There were seventeen dump truck loads. I later learned there had been another shakedown a few years before with almost the same results.

So while a busted pipe wouldn't have been appreciated in most cell houses, a flash flood inside A-Hall was a real disaster.

At seventy pounds of pressure, a one-inch pipe can dump a lot of water in a hurry. As I desperately tried to think of something to stop the flow of water, Cuddle Bear began to let me know he had a lot of influence, or *juice*, as he called it, and would see me fired if I didn't get the water stopped. When that didn't work, he threatened me with a lawsuit. I hadn't worked at the pen too long before I got used to hearing "I'll hang a writ on you," or "I'll take you to court and own everything you have," so I wasn't too upset over the threats, but I did want to get the water shut off.

Against Cuddle Bear's protests, I left the cell and headed to the ground floor to shut the water off with a valve. Cuddle Bear's cell was on the top floor, and already water was cascading down from one tier to the next and landing on two of the four pool tables that sat on the flag area of the bottom floor. I climbed down the eight flights of steps and turned the corner onto the flag. It was quiet, and a dozen cold stares greeted me. I got the distinct feeling that at that moment I was possibly not the A-Hall inmates' favorite staff member.

Killing the water at the flag shut off eight cells, and normally I would have taken time to inform everyone in those cells that the water was going off. This time I just hurried into the waterfall and began cranking the valve. Normally, the valves are hard to spin, but this one was turning easily. I kept spinning it around and around, but nothing changed, and with a sinking feeling, I realized the valve was no good.

Even so, I kept turning the valve so it would appear I was doing something while I tried to remember if I had ever been shown the cut-off valve for the entire housing unit. Finally, I went to the sergeant's office to use the phone. The officer was leaning against the windowsill, smoking a cigarette and looking across the yard. I told him I needed to use the phone.

Without turning his head he said, "Go ahead. I seen you had some trouble out there. Kind of stirred up a hornet's nest, didn't you?"

I was hoping he was looking out the window instead of watching the growing mob because he was confident that the inmates weren't going to attack me, but I was afraid he knew the paperwork would be a lot simpler for finding a dead man than for seeing how the man became deceased. I got the phone, called M&M, and asked Bill Wieberg to call down to the plumbing shop and see if someone could come over to A-Hall and show me where to shut off the water. Ed Hanauer showed up a few minutes later, looked at the new indoor swimming pool and the dazzling, cascading waterfalls creating it and asked, "Having troubles?"

When I told him that I had broken a pipe on the top floor and needed the water shut off, he pointed out the valve I had been turning and said, "There's the valve that feeds it. Just turn it off."

Having spent enough time inside MSP to know I didn't want to live there, I fought off a sudden murderous impulse and responded, "I'm not quite as stupid as I look. That valve doesn't work. I need to know where to kill the water to the whole house."

Still unperturbed—after all, it was me and not him who had the inmates irritated—Hanauer sent an inmate back to M&M to get a four-foot-long water key. In the meantime, he took me out in front of the housing unit and began kicking around on the ground until he kicked up a metal cover. When the inmate got back with the key, they stuck it down in the ground and turned the water off. Relieved, I went back in the housing unit.

My relief didn't last long. I was horrified to see inmates com-

All of the trash on the floor is contraband that was found in cells
in A-Hall during a search and lockdown operation entitled "Spring
Cleaning" in April 1992.

ing up out of the shower area with soap all over their heads. These
inmates were hollering, but stopped when some of the other inmates
pointed toward me. I'm sure those inmates were explaining what a
good worker I was and how hard I was trying. Soon the showering
inmates started towards me. Not wanting to be embarrassed by their
praise, I quickly ran up the steps to Cuddle Bear's cell.

As I worked to fix the broken pipe, Cuddle Bear loudly
informed me of all the property that I had ruined and how he
was certain I wanted to pay for it all. Finally, I finished up and
got out of there. As I was leaving the housing unit, some of the
inmates were still mopping up. One inmate looked at me as he
rolled a ball across a saturated pool table; the ball sent up of walls
of spray. Without a word, I slipped on out the door.

Noah got a rainbow, but I received no such promise as
I walked out of the great flood of A-Hall. I knew as long as I
worked at MSP, I faced the chance of disaster.

Chapter 19

The MSP Burrito Bandits

Many times at MSP, I had an angry inmate remind me that the riot in the fifties started because of bad food. Inmates griped about the food continuously, with common complaints being that it had no taste, tasted like crap, was inedible, had been contaminated, and—the most common complaint—that inmates weren't given enough of it.

Staff was served the same food, cooked at the same time in the same kitchen. Many of them also complained about the free food. Personally, I had carried my lunch and eaten either in a truck cab or sitting on a pile of lumber for too many years to complain about sitting in a chair at a table and having a hot lunch served on a plate, plus someone to clean off the table and do the dishes when I was finished. It may not have been the best tasting food in the world, but it sure beat a cold bologna sandwich all to pieces.

I discussed this once with a disgruntled inmate. At first he denied the food was ever edible, but finally he admitted that most days, two out of three meals weren't too bad. But then he added, "How would you like to have to eat this food every day and never go out somewhere to eat?" I told him my attitude was a lot of poor folks would be glad to have it and would not complain, and I didn't think people locked up for committing crimes ought to be treated better or have more than the poorest taxpayer. Somehow, that attitude and the fact that I was willing to share my feelings did not endear me to the inmate.

One thing I will admit, and it made a lot of people think twice before eating (others thought twice and then didn't eat),

is that sometimes there were things in the food that were not
supposed to be there. That is to say there were items that might
wind up in the cuisine that the kitchen staff did not have on their
ingredient list, things that would never have been in a recipe
book. There were always rumors of inmates urinating or defecat-
ing in the food, but that would have been extremely rare if it ever
actually happened at all. For that kind of inmate, if found out,
would not survive long enough to try it again. More common
complaints were inmates washing their clothes in the dishwashers
or steam pots, and at least once an inmate was caught bathing in
a steam pot. Once in a great while, a mouse or possibly a cock-
roach might be present, but it was always cooked properly.

I'm sure there was a certain amount of contamination in the
food, but the same inmates who did the cooking also ate the food
and tried to steal a fair amount of it to sell in the housing units.
The last thing they wanted was to eat, or sell, contaminated food.
I worked in a couple of restaurants when I was a teenager, and
I know what goes on in the back of the kitchen. If you're squeamish, eat at home. If you do eat out, try not to think about it. As
for me, I'll take good old inmate-prepared prison food any day.

Food was continually being stolen or misappropriated
(depending on who was doing the stealing) at MSP in the 1980s.
There were rules about food: Some things were approved, some
were allowed, some were prohibited, and some could cost a staff
person his or her job. But the problem was, no one knew which
actions fell into which categories. One notable exception was a
rule for the officer in the staff dining room. He was never to let
the cafeteria run out of bacon before Warden Donald Wyrick got
his breakfast. I was there one time when that happened. It was
not a pretty sight, nor was it safe for bystanders. I never saw the
dining room empty so fast.

There were many situations outside of mealtime where
staff felt free to help themselves to food. Back when I was a labor
foreman at the start of my MSP career, one of the first things I did

when I got to M&M in the morning was to walk the tool room's
inmate worker up to the kitchen to get coffee. At some time in
the past, someone had taken a three-gallon milk can and out-
fitted it with a spigot like what's found on a garden hose faucet.
The inmate and I would take a two-wheeled dolly and this milk
can to the main kitchen, where morning coffee was made in a
fifty-gallon pot. We would drain some of the leftover, four-hour-
old coffee into our milk can and hurry back to M&M before the
coffee could get cold.

Perhaps you have heard of coffee that would float a horseshoe? This coffee wouldn't do that, but I bet it would have taken a
horseshoe ten minutes to drift to the bottom. I watched in amazement as the inmates and even some of the staff drank this brew.
Occasionally, a whippersnapper inmate would drain out a cup
of this potent drink and attempt to down it all nonchalant-like,
like the old cons. A stiffening of facial muscles, quick blinking,
streaming tears, and a quivering of the throat were the immediate
response. Some minutes later, a twisting of the insides would run
the inmate off to the bathroom, where recovery was slow and
painful.

On the other hand, the kitchen's cinnamon rolls, made from
scratch each Friday, were fit for a king. When we got the coffee,
we would bring a large tray of those rolls back to M&M. There
were more than enough for everyone to have one, and I even
tried to have a little coffee with mine one time.

Another place staff and inmates found food was in the cold
storage area, which had its own stove. It was amazing how many
people had business down there. I began to understand why
so many of the older staff members were as hefty as they were.
Someone would fire up the stove and get the skillet hot; then they
would fry up a few confiscated eggs and a chunk of confiscated
beef (raised at another Missouri penitentiary, Church Farm),
toast some bread on a steam pipe, and several staff members
would eat their fill. This would be between breakfast (where these

same people had eaten) and lunch (when they would eat again). Then at about three o'clock, these same people would be up at the staff dining room to eat the evening meal before heading home for supper.

Back in those days, the inmate food service workers also made ice cream in the cold storage area and boxed it up in half-gallon containers. The kitchen would serve it about once a month. One time the prison was locked down due to a hostage situation while my inmate workers and I were working on a freezer drain. The cold storage supervisor broke out the ice cream, and we ate for two solid hours.

Back then, two or three times a week, MSP baked bread, and the enticing aroma greeted all who entered. On many frosty winter morns, I found myself in the bakery with hundreds of loaves of fresh-from-the-oven bread. Butter in pound packages would be on the counter, and an uncut loaf of bread would be torn apart, smothered with butter, and devoured in a manner to make witnesses believe my crew and I were all starving to death.

Once the whole plumbing shop was on the kitchen dock when a truckload of commodity cheese was being unloaded. The cheese was in three-pound packages, six packages to a box, and it was being stacked along a wall that went down towards cold storage. At that time, the back of the dock held hot water boilers in a cage and a door going into Tunnel 3. That part of the dock area was called K-4. Workers from both the plumbing shop and the machine shop were working in that area, and two big shots from administration were there to inspect the work being done. I noticed one of the inmates swipe a box of cheese and hide it in the tunnel. I went to where Ed Hanauer was standing and was starting to explain the situation to him when another box of cheese went by and Hanauer cautioned the inmate to be sure to put it where the kitchen staff could not see it from the door. I moved back close to one of the big shots and began talking to him. I figured that when this situation blew up, I could tell him

I had had no part in it and could remind him I had been talking to him at the time. Not long after I made this wise decision, the machine shop foreman noticed what was happening and came up to the other side of the same big shot.

"Hey!" the machine shop foreman cried. "Do you see what the plumbing shop is doing? They're stealing boxes of cheese!"

To which the big shot responded, "Shut up. One of those is for me."

For the inmates, access to extra food meant access to an extra source of income. Inmates who worked in the kitchen and dining rooms were allowed (unofficially) to fill their pockets with sandwiches (usually wrapped in food service gloves) and augment their meager salaries by selling them in their housing units. Others stole the things that were not so plentiful, such as canned juice, in a million clever ways. Once, while staff was shaking down my inmate workers as we were leaving the storage area, one of the inmates who worked in the commissary pushed a mop bucket full of dirty water past us and into the bathroom. A few moments later as I walked by, I glanced in and saw this inmate lifting cans of orange juice out of the mop bucket. Another inmate put peanut butter in a food service glove, put the filled glove in his shoe, and tried to walk out of the kitchen. He was caught when someone noticed his shoes were oozing peanut butter laces.

Somehow leftover pancake batter (along with butter and syrup) would wind up in A-Hall—the housing unit with the posh cells and high level of inmate freedom—and a restaurant would spring up. The proprietors wouldn't take American Express, but if you had yard books—which contained prison coupons for shopping in the commissary—or cigarettes, you could leave with a plate full of hotcakes, cooked on a gallon can turned upside down over a three hundred-watt lightbulb. This was all contraband, of course, but the first time I saw the operation, the housing unit's officer was the fifth customer in line. With clientele like that, the inmates didn't fret too much about being written up for breaking prison rules.

This kind of "freethinking" about MSP food ended when an illicit burrito shop was given a little too much assistance from the staff. It had never been too unusual for the cold storage area or the dry and canned food area to be raided by the evening shift, but the theft had never been a big deal—until, that is, the burrito shop was set up in one of the quaint residences of the prosperous A-Hall neighborhood. Word soon got out that the inmate running it could really cook. As more and more of the staff visited this little business, it began to be very difficult for the proprietor to stock his meager cupboard and the staff began to help him. In order for him to turn a profit, he had to have enough goods to sell to the inmate population; staff members did not pay for their meals except by providing ingredients. It turns out that when people find an eating establishment where the food is outstanding and free, they will go to great lengths to keep it operating.

Eventually, as staff and A-Hall inmates were kept well-fed and the pockets of the cook bulged, it became more and more difficult for the real MSP kitchen to keep in stock the ingredients also needed in the burrito shop. Meals had to be substituted and some were cooked without seasoning (I'm pretty sure I ate some of those). The problem became so great that the central office finally investigated, and the vast number and the ranks of those involved was staggering. The situation called for drastic changes in the rules, and even more drastic changes in enforcement of the rules. Several people even lost their jobs, including, if I remember right, a captain and a sergeant.

We called it The Great Burrito Caper and ever after, the inmate culprits were known to MSP staff as the Burrito Bandits. Their exploits forever changed the way food was misappropriated at the Missouri State Penitentiary.

Chapter 20

Troublesome Twins

One of my favorite parts of working in MSP was getting to work in the historic structures. I've always loved history, and the MSP buildings connected me to many decades passed. But just like a homeowner who decides it will be fun to fix up a quaint old house, I came to realize that historic architecture can be a major challenge to maintain. Take, for example, the MSP Housing Units 2 and 5.

These two housing units were twins, both built in 1938 on the same plan except for two extra bottom floors in Housing Unit 5. Both housing units were called lever halls because of the mechanism used to open the cell doors. There was an ingenious system for dialing the door or doors to be opened, then pulling down on a long lever that could actually open up to twenty-one doors at a time. It took a bit of a pull to open that many doors, and because of the system's age and dilapidation it seldom worked correctly. This caused much frustration, and the perturbed officers heaped abuse upon the poor old dials and levers, causing further dilapidation and more miscues, which caused even more frustration. I have seen newer officers be upset almost to tears, while many of the old hands worked the mechanisms easily, aware of the system's quirks and surly disposition.

No outside business manufactured parts for the contraption anymore so the machine shop was often busy welding, rebuilding, or manufacturing replacement parts, from small catches and flat receivers called shoes to the long operating handles. This repair work ran in cycles, notably coinciding with staff changes in those two housing units.

The lever box in Housing Unit 2-B in 1968, several years before Neal almost broke it. Photo from the collection of Mark Schreiber.

Because of the complexity and fragility of the antique working parts, few people were allowed to work on the system. I had only limited time in the machine shop and none in the lock shop, so I had never been involved in helping with repairs, not even to take the covers off. Then one day in the late nineties, I was called in after hours to get a jammed cell door open in Housing Unit 2. Staff had called the locksmith, former lock shop employees, and machine shop personnel, all without getting ahold of anyone. Finally in desperation, they had called me. Because no one else seemed to be available, I believed it would be all right for me to try to fix it. I brought in the security screwdriver and removed the cover screws, and then, with the hall sergeant looking over my shoulder, began to try to remove the cover.

The bracket that held the cover on was stuck. The hall sergeant was fidgeting, concerned that something might happen that would require getting the inmates out in a hurry, like a fire. The longer we took, the more he fretted. I pulled and pried and jerked and studied, but I just could not figure out how to get the cover bracket loose. I then told the sergeant that I was going back to M&M to get a bigger pry bar. At that point he said that he probably didn't know any more than I did, but he thought there was a lock in the lever box that had to be removed to get the covers off.

We went and looked, and he pointed out a lock in the upper right-hand corner. He said that if he remembered right, the last time they had worked on it, they took that lock off first. We were unable to locate the key, so I wound up cutting the lock off. I was sure hoping that sergeant knew what he was talking about and that I wasn't going to make things worse and maybe get the whole line jammed up. After we got the lock off, the cover easily came off. Silently, I breathed a prayer of gratitude that I had not succeeded in prying the cover loose like I had been trying to do. After examining the workings for a few minutes, I realized what a brilliantly simple mechanism it really was. I found the problem and temporarily repaired it. The next day I told the locksmith what I had done and what I had tried to do. He nearly went into a fit when I told him how hard I had pried on the cover.

Like most of the housing units, Housing Units 2 and 5 had plumbing tunnels in their centers, with cells on either side. Outside the cells was an open space to windows. The plumbing tunnels in Housing Units 2 and 5 were much narrower than those in Housing Unit 3, and the plumbing tighter and harder to get to. The tunnel was not open to the basement but ended on the cell house level with office areas below. That was a dumb idea. Even dumber was a lack of a walkway on the bottom level. Pipes ran across about four feet high every ten feet or so and had to be climbed over, and there was also knee-high plumbing every three or four feet that had to be negotiated. It was a nightmare to drag a box full of tools and parts to the end of the tunnel to fix a plumbing problem.

Often when a problem required working both in a cell and in the tunnel behind the cell, I would lock the plumbing inmates in the tunnel, and then I would work in the cell. First I had to find the walk officer and ask him to "throw that cell off-line," which meant dial that cell, open it, and then unselect it; it would stay open until I pulled it shut upon leaving or until the officer forgot and dialed it back in for some reason. Often I would be working on a faucet or perhaps pulling a toilet when I would hear a rattling, a click, and all of the doors on the walk would open; then all of them would be pulled shut, including mine. The first few times it was rather unnerving, but eventually I got used to it. There was no way to get the officer's attention, so I'd shout through the wall to the inmates in the plumbing tunnel, telling them that we were stuck. Usually I'd sit on the bed and look for a book to read or watch television until someone found us.

The convicts in the tunnel, however, were easily bored and would go to the end of the tunnel and bang on the door to get someone's attention. If we weren't on the flag, they might climb down and bang on the flag tunnel door asking to be let out. Once in a while it worked. The longest I was locked in a cell was three hours, and it was getting close to quitting time when they finally found me. I had just gone to look at a leak to see if it really was a leak, so I didn't have any inmates with me that time. If the toilet was flushed a lot on a hot humid day, condensation would build up and drip off the bottom of the commode and onto the floor. The cell's occupant would always believe his toilet had started leaking and desperately want it fixed. I had found it to be a good idea to check out a potentially leaking toilet before I brought the whole crew over.

The outsides of the buildings were brick and the insides of the lower levels were masonry, but up in the halls, everything was built of quarter-inch sheet metal fastened together with boiler rivets. The cells were too small to be used for two men, and the single legless beds were fastened back-to-back to the same

metal wall. This resulted in all of the motion of a large convict in
his bunk being transferred to the next room where it bounced
a smaller inmate up and down in his bunk all night. For years,
contraband wooden blocks were packed into the cells and used as
legs to hold up a bunk and stop the motion. Eventually concerns
about a possible fire hazard resulted in requiring that all wood
be removed from the prison cells. When this was rigorously
enforced, not even allowing for reasonable exceptions, many of
these prisoners lost their only possibility of a good night's sleep.
This in turn caused many of them to be more difficult to control
and much more ready to engage in fights and other disturbances.

Looking for a way to vent their frustrations, unhappy
inmates often turned to their toilets to work off aggression.
Blankets, coats, and even shoes were forced down the throat of a
poor, innocent, unsuspecting toilet and into the vile trunk lines
where such foreign objects would hang up and refuse passage
to elements that actually had a right to use the pipes. The main
other egress for all the backed-up water was the toilets in the cells
on either side, where it would pour out and flood the cell before
escaping out onto the walkways and down to the flag area, in
stunning but sometimes lumpy waterfalls. If an inmate was in his
cell, he could keep his toilet from flooding by continually flushing
it, but of course, this added to the total amount of water coming
out of someone else's cell.

Usually by the time the plumbing shop would arrive to
view the disaster, the hallway was reverberating with the din of
screaming inmates who, between standing on their beds and constantly flushing their toilets, were hurling unprintable insults and
threats to every other inmate who continued to flush his toilet. If
the convicts had already been discontented, other walks would
join in by stopping up their sewer pipes, then flushing their toilets
and screaming. Although the resulting flood was usually confined
to the walks actually doing the flooding and the flag below, on at
least one occasion the flooding was so bad that water was run-

ning out the front doors of the unit in a vibrant rolling stream.

This created quite a problem for the plumbers who had to enter the flooded tunnels to make repairs. Yet in spite of the fact that the tunnels would be flooded with the sewer pipe contents, it was worse for those who had to work in the offices directly under the plumbing tunnels. Before we would even arrive in the housing unit, the overflow would be making its way down through the cracks in the tunnel floor and into the office areas below. Housing Units 2 and 5 had a "complex," or office area for caseworkers, in the basement. It would usually take a week for the tunnels to dry out from a flood, so we would continue to get calls from the soggy areas below complaining of water leaks, but there was nothing we could do. Once the hall sergeant had the porters try to mop the tunnel floor, but the vast array of piping and conduit at varying heights, much of it near the floor, made it impossible to get much of the water swabbed up.

And the flooding wasn't a new problem when I arrived. Mark Schreiber recalled that sometime around 1969 he was teaching in a classroom in the lower level of Housing Unit 5 when the flooding got so bad he had to wear a raincoat. "This was when integration was being attempted, and the inmates flooded the units for days," Schreiber said. "The water was several inches deep and ran down the steps outside Housing Unit 5."

Over in Housing Unit 2, much of the water that came down from the intermittent floods fell into the area housing the huge transformer that supplied power to the unit, and the engineering staff was constantly amazed that this high-voltage transformer did not explode. In the last few months of MSP, engineers from the Office of Administration came to see which buildings could be saved and what would have to be done to save them. I showed them this transformer and saw for the first time that the conduit feeding the power from this area up to the hall had corroded so badly that much of the wire inside was actually exposed. When the inspectors saw this, almost invariably they would shudder, shake their heads, and call to any other inspectors with them who hadn't seen it to come over and look. Then they would murmur in low tones while shaking their heads at the conduit and glance at me like it was all my fault.

When MSP closed, Housing Units 2 and 5 had each seen more than seventy years of service and had housed thousands of men. These buildings survived the riot of 1954 and a failed attempt to desegregate the inmates in the 1960s. And as I write this, those units have so far escaped the wrecking ball. But even if such a fate befalls them, these twins will forever stand in the memories of those who lived and worked at MSP.

Chapter 21

Memories of Housing Unit 3

I still remember taking in the grandeur of Housing Unit 3 the first time I saw it. I love the look of limestone buildings, and Housing Unit 3 was castle-like. The building was four stories tall, and the entrance stood between two round towers topped with crenellation. The towers rose above the roofline and were commonly mistaken for gun towers, but really, they were just airshafts that supplied outside air to the ancient and mostly abandoned basement heating machinery. From the towers' sides stretched two identical halls with repeating stripes of limestone and dark, towering banks of windows.

Stepping inside Housing Unit 3, the wing to the right was 3-A and 3-B was the wing to the left. There were four levels to each of these wings, and the bottom level had a concrete slab floor. Below this floor was another full level, 3-C, and in 1984, it housed death row on one side and "the hole," a punitive area where prisoners were sent for short time periods, on the other. The side with the hole had one more level lower still, 3-D, also called O-Hall, which housed mentally ill inmates who were heavily medicated.

Back up above in 3-A and 3-B, the center of each level had one long tunnel that served as a plumbing access. These tunnels were about five feet wide with about two and a half feet of walking room between the plumbing. The walkways of the tunnels were made of vertical steel slats, spaced about an inch apart, and connected by rods. When you looked down, you could see straight through to the lower levels. It was a lot like standing on nothing.

A view of Housing Unit 3 during the time Neal worked at MSP. Housing Unit 3 opened in 1914.

On each side of the plumbing tunnel were the cellblocks. On the bottom floor, the approximately twelve feet between the cell blocks and the outside wall was all open; this was called the "flag." Looking up from the flag, you could see the three higher levels of cellblocks, each wrapped with a walkway lined with a three-pipe rail.

The housing unit's huge banks of windows reached from the floor to the ceiling. There was a strange combination of ancient levers, gears, and rods that at one time had been a clever method of opening the windows from the flag. By my time, the convicts used these defunct contraptions as ladders to open the windows by hand. Each hall sergeant tried to hire at least one inmate walkman who was not afraid to climb to the ceiling to open or close the windows. I can still remember one stormy summer day when driving sheets of rain were blowing in through the windows, and several inmates, their clothing whipping around them, were climbing and clinging to these rods and bars while struggling to close the windows against the rain and wind. In that moment, I was no longer

The administrative segregation area known as "The Hole" was located on the back side of Housing Unit 3-C, under 3-B. Neal helped to wheelbarrow in the concrete to make the cells' bunks.

inside MSP but on a raging sea, watching a band of pirates cling to
their ship's rigging while struggling to lower the sails in a wicked
oceanic storm.

The Housing Unit 3 plumbing tunnels, like the plumbing tunnels elsewhere in the pen, were ancient and dilapidated.
About every fifteen feet, there was a bare lightbulb mounted to
the catwalk above, but at least half of these were usually burned
out. At least the tunnels' steel-slat walkways allowed light to enter
from levels above, while lights below cast weird shadows on the
pipes and walls. Numerous pinhole leaks in the plumbing sprayed
a barely visible mist onto the plastered limestone walls, where the
water ran down and created strange formations from the calcium
and other minerals in the prison's well water. Much of the leaking
plumbing fittings also had a thick crust of limestone. In some
places there was so much limestone on the plumbing and walls
that the tunnel looked more like a cave than a building.

Along with plumbing, the tunnels had old electric wires
that had at some time furnished the cells with 110-volt electric
lights. The wires ran on insulators, suggesting the wiring predated
Romex and conduit. Even when MSP was closed in 2004, the only
lights in the cells were uncovered 75-watt bulbs in porcelain pull-
chain fixtures, and the single most commonly reported electrical
problem in the whole institution was light fixtures with missing
or broken pull chains.

The Housing Unit 3 plumbing tunnels also contained abandoned speaker wires connected to little boxes that, I was told, had
at one time piped two radio stations into the cells. The convicts
could choose which of the two to listen to or could choose to
have neither. This was back when no radios or TVs had been
allowed in the cells.

Starting in the late 1970s or early 1980s, death row inmates—
who were kept locked in their cells 24/7 except for exercise—were
allowed to have cable TV. One of the first things I learned in the
plumbing shop was that the twenty-four-hour inmate plumber had

a hustle that I was not to interfere with. For fifty dollars, he would splice into the cable TV co-ax line and run cable TV to a cell up in Housing Unit 3-A. These splices were not done with connectors and splitters, but in true convict fashion the wire was stripped back to bare the center connector, where a piece of co-ax, salvaged from discarded pieces on the floor, was taped in and bandaged up with black tape. If black tape was unavailable, it would be sealed with masking tape or even occasionally with Scotch tape. Usually at least two, sometimes several, pieces of co-ax were then connected end-to-end to reach the cell where the new customer lived.

Each illicit tap caused a certain amount of deterioration in the signal strength in death row, and after enough contraband subscribers had been hooked up, the maintenance man in charge of phone service would have to disconnect everything. He would complain bitterly to Ed Hanauer about the plumbing inmates' involvement. Hanauer would laugh at him, deny any knowledge of the cable business, and in the same breath explain that an inmate couldn't survive without some kind of a hustle unless he worked for Missouri Vocational Enterprises, which included the factories. Even many of the MVE workers ran a hustle. At that time, convicts paid for almost everything they got, whether it was contraband or (supposed to be) state issue. The phone man did not do the work himself; he had an inmate helper who undoubt-edly had been paid not to unhook certain cells, as some were never disconnected. This inmate also dropped all the unhooked cable back down to the floor of the tunnel, and, unless I am mistaken, occasionally dropped long pieces of new cable to the floor. I also know that sometimes, when staff had this inmate out at night to repair a plumbing problem, he would con the escort-ing officer into taking him into the phone room to get extra co-ax cable. He lost his hustle in the late 1980s when cable TV was installed throughout the institution.

Each tunnel level had its own door, but once inside, the inmates climbed with ease from one level to another; I couldn't help but think of monkeys swinging in the jungle. The catwalks were in the middle of the tunnel, with the sewer and water lines against each wall. By climbing on the pipes, the inmates could go up or down. The first time I saw them doing it, I was sure they were going to fall and kill or cripple themselves, which would get me into a lot of trouble. The pipes and conduit gave them plenty of hand- and footholds, and the next catwalk level was only about

Inside a plumbing tunnel in Housing Unit 3 just weeks before MSP's closing. There is more space than it appears; there was room on the sides for the plumbing crew to climb up and down the pipes, although it was a tight squeeze.

nine feet down, but the floor beneath them was anywhere from twenty to sixty feet down. After a few months in the plumbing shop, I was making the trip up and down with them.

We also climbed up and down the tunnels in Housing Units 2 and 5. Those were a much tighter fit, but to compensate for the tight squeeze, there was a lot more broken—but still hot—

electric conduit for us to hang onto. I never had but one broken
conduit to short out, and it didn't burn me. It just knocked out the
lights in most of the cells. It also made the tunnel lights go out. My
feet couldn't reach the catwalk and I couldn't find a handhold, so I
finally had to jump towards where I knew the catwalk had to be. I
was right and hit it just right, but it was a weird feeling as I dropped.

Up in the attic of Housing Unit 3 we had to be careful where
we stepped. To get up there, we had to climb a pipe ladder from
the top tunnel catwalk, then hang onto the ladder while unlocking and opening the trap door into the attic. The floor of the area
above the tunnel was made of chain-link fencing, which was
both difficult and unsafe to stand on. The area over the cells was
concrete and the area over the flag area four stories below was
plaster—which I once proved would not support a person.

Bill Wieberg had sent me up in the attic to see if the down-
spouts could be accessed from inside, and as I started to walk
across the ceiling, suddenly my foot went through. I hadn't
realized in the dark gloom that the concrete had ended and I was
walking on plaster. I pulled my leg out of the hole and looked
down through the remnants of drifting plaster at inmates staring
up at me from the flag four stories down. My stomach knotted
up, and I gingerly crawled back to solid footing. When I got back
to M&M and told Wieberg what I had done, he looked at me,
surprised and alarmed, and said, "You can't walk on that ceiling!"

To which I replied, "I know that *now!*"

In the attic, there was another pipe ladder leading up to the
roof through another trap door. Once up on the roof, a person
could scoot down to the parapets and look down on the people
far below.

One time I had to climb up onto one of the towers to replace
a stone that lightning had knocked off. To someone on the ground,
those stones did not look all that big when in their rightful positions. But looks can be deceiving, as I realized when I examined
the fallen stone on the ground. Picking it up proved to be too much

for even two men. The maintenance supervisor over me gave me a work order to place the stone back on the tower. Considering the weight and size of the rock and the route to the top of the building, I asked him how I was supposed to accomplish this feat. He told me that it was my problem and that he expected me to find a way. One day a crane was brought in to work on the roof of Housing Unit 1 and I convinced the operators, through the fine art of groveling, to pause long enough to pick up the stone and put it back in place on top of four one-inch nuts.

That was step one. Step two was mudding the rock back into place. Heights don't affect me as badly as they do some people, but anything over three stories does something to my legs. They felt as wobbly as Jell-O as I sat down on the top edge of that tower, but the convict working with me sat in one of the gaps between the rocks and leaned out far enough to mud in the seam under the front of the stone. I, meanwhile, sat in the same space and leaned the opposite direction while holding onto his belt. I don't mean to suggest that would have done any good had he started to lose his balance, but it was our only safety equipment back then. It was my job to hold his belt. It was his job not to slip. I figured that if he didn't do his job, then he couldn't complain if I didn't do mine. At least he couldn't have complained very long.

Another time the sewer line from 3-D, also called O-Hall, was stopped up. By that time, I had been working in the plumbing shop for years and thought I had been everywhere, so I was surprised when Hanauer revealed a trapdoor out by the road that gave access to the waste and steam supply piping. Once I was in this crawl space, I discovered that it led back under the floor of 3-D. It truly was a crawl space as it was only about twenty inches high and two feet wide, and I had to crawl back several feet to reach the end. I only went under there the one time, but that was enough. I can now boast that from the top of the highest to the bottom of the lowest, I experienced the full measure of Housing Unit 3.

Chapter 22

An Unlikely Friendship

His name was Alberto Garcia, and I felt sorry for him.

He was one of my inmate workers in the MSP plumbing shop, and one look at him showed he was beaten down. He walked with shoulders bowed, head down, and feet dragging. Whenever he looked up, his eyes were constantly darting about, as though he always expected attack. Originally from Cuba, he spoke in broken English—that is, when he spoke at all, which was rare. He did what he was told to do without argument but also without a bit of interest.

One day when I had a job to do in a plumbing tunnel of Housing Unit 3, I told Garcia to grab some tools and come with me. As we went, I prayed that somehow I could reach him, perhaps help him, but at least be his friend.

When we were in the tunnel and had sat down on the catwalk to work on a flushometer for a cell commode, I decided to attempt some small talk.

"You know, I've always wanted to learn to speak Spanish," I said. "Do you think maybe you could teach me a few words?"

Garcia grunted and shrugged his shoulders.

I held up a pair of channel locks and said, "*Pliers*. How do you say?"

"*Pinciers.*"

"*Pinchers?*"

"No, no. You no say right. *Pinciers.*"

That was the most I had ever heard him speak, so I tried again. "*Pinchiers?*"

This time I got a small smile, a nod, and a shrugging of his shoulders. I took it to mean, "Pretty close." I turned off the valve for the water to the toilet and said, "Inside the pipe is water. How do you say *water*?"

"*Agua.*"

"*Aug-wah*?"

This time a bigger smile, more nodding of the head, and, "Si, si, *agua.*"

As I took the top off and some water spilled out, I said, "That's cold. How do you say *cold*?"

"*Frío.*"

"*Free-oh*?"

Again a nodding of the head and a smile.

"O.K.," I went on, "*Hot*. How do you say *hot*?"

"*Caliente.*"

"*Call-e-on-tee*?"

"No. No. You no say right, you crazy American. *Caliente.*" His English words came out rough and broken. The Spanish flowed like water in a brook. There was no way I could imitate him. But I tried.

"*Call-le-en-tee*?"

This time he actually laughed.

"No. No. Is not the way you say. Is *caliente.*"

Encouraged at seeing him opening up a bit, I said, "I wonder, how does this place compare to Cuban prisons? Are Cuban prisons like this?"

"No, no," he said, his smile fading. "Cuban prison not like American at all. In Cuba, one big room, like this big—" he indicated from one end of the tunnel to the other, about 150 feet. "Maybe three hundred men inside. We no go to dining room; we eat there. They bring food and set inside door, then lock, and everyone fight for food."

Appalled, I asked, "Do they give you plates and bowls, or what do you eat on?"

"They no give anything," he answered casually. "You maybe take piece of wood and you make bowl. You scoop out."

He emphasized with hand motions the whittling of the wood into a plate or bowl.

"How do you whittle?" I asked, surprised. "Did you have knives?"

"Everyone have knife," he answered. "You make knife first when you get there. You need for eat; you need for fight."

"Do many people get stabbed?"

"Si," he said, gloomily. "Many. Many stab, many kill. Every day, many."

I was fascinated. "Did you have toilets like these in the bathrooms?" I asked, and he surprised me with a laugh.

"No, no," he said. "Is no toilets, no room, is buckets. Maybe two, maybe three."

"Did you ever go out for recreation, for exercise?"

Again, he laughed. "No, no. No good food. No, how you say, exercise." He looked me straight in the face and said, "Me like American prison!"

I was surprised at how easy it was to get him to share with me, and I began to ask about his home and his family. He told me his father was in the military and, I gathered, had a high rank. I asked Garcia if he had ever seen Fidel Castro, and he said that Castro had been to his house many times to sit and talk with his father. He said that his mother's father had come from Germany and that his mother worked for Castro as a translator and could speak English, German, Russian, and Chinese. Matter-of-factly, like it should come as no surprise to me, he told me that he could also speak German. Some of the inmates had been making fun of him because of his broken English, and all the while, he could speak two languages well and another well enough to be understood.

I asked how he had ended up in a Cuban prison, and he told me he had an older brother who had been sent to fight in Angola and had come back alive but "all full of holes." Then their uncle tried to send Garcia and he refused.

"I say, 'I no go. I no fight. I no want to be all full of holes.'
My uncle, he say, 'You go to prison!' I say, 'Me go to prison. Me
no go to Angola and come home all full of holes.'"

Garcia and I continued to talk until we finished our work,
and from that day on, he never had a problem talking with me.
I began to take him with me on all of my jobs—sometimes just
him, sometimes with others—and he began to show an eagerness
to go and to learn how to repair the plumbing and the steam.
Nobody ever showed an eagerness to learn about the sewers, but
he was willing to do what was needed. Soon, his willingness to
talk to me extended to the others in the plumbing shop, and he
found acceptance among the other inmates.

One day, a few months after our first conversation, Garcia was
called to see his caseworker. He came back in a state of panic. The
caseworker had said he had to sign papers to go back to Cuba or
he would be locked up in a punitive unit. His eyes were red and
rimmed with tears, and he was shaking.

"I no go," he said. "Castro would kill. Castro would torture
and kill, and I no go."

I told him no one could make him sign papers saying he
wanted to go back, but he acted as if he wasn't listening.

"They put me on a plane, I jump out. I no go back. I jump in
the ocean."

The caseworker tried a few more times to make him sign
saying that he wanted to go back. Many of the Cubans were being
sent back, probably a lot of them against their will, but eventually,
Garcia was left alone.

About a year later, Garcia and I were working in a cell when he
pulled out a couple of photos and showed them to me. I saw a

little boy and a little girl—his children, he told me.

"Those are a couple of good-looking kids," I said. "Especially that girl. She's a doll."

He smiled, proud.

"Are they in Cuba?" I asked.

"No, no. These are my American kids."

Once again, he had surprised me. "You had kids in America?"

"Si. I work for contractor in St. Louis. I meet good-looking girl. She Mexican. We get married and buy house and have kids. Good kids." He was looking at the photos, and watching him, I got a lump in my throat. I wondered how I'd handle not getting to see my daughters except when someone might bring them for a visit.

Swallowing hard I asked, "Does your wife bring them to visit you very often?"

There was silence for a few moments as he gently touched the little girl's face.

"No. When I arrested, she take kids and leave. I never see no more. I no know where they go. I never see again."

I didn't know what to say, and I doubt I could have spoken anyway. All I could think was, "What if I could never see my girls again?" He looked at the photos, head bowed, shoulders slumped, tears filling his eyes. Then, ever so gently, he put the photos away. Quietly, we finished our work, and I silently prayed for God to heal his hurt and help this lonely man. Without a word, we picked up the tools and went back to the shop.

Despite his hardships, Garcia turned out to be a great one for laughs. Many of his tales about life in Cuba were humorous, and how he told them, with animated facial expressions and lots of hand waving, made his stories hilarious. He didn't mind that we often laughed when he didn't mean to be funny. He'd just get a silly grin on his face as he waited to be let in on the joke.

One of my favorite stories he told was about his time in the Cuban military. After his uncle had been unsuccessful in getting him to join up, his father had forced him into it.

"They put me in army, and I no happy," he told me. "I no like army life. Then they give me rifle. I no like army, but I like gun."

"I bet!" I said with a laugh.

Garcia smiled. "They put me on guard," he continued, "and they say to me, 'You see something move, you yell, "Halt!" If they no halt, if they no answer, you shoot.' Me happy. Me like gun. Me want to shoot gun. Me watch. Me no see something, but me want to shoot gun! Me shoot! Brrraaaappp!" Garcia mimed shooting. "They come running. They say, 'You see something?' Me say, 'Si! It move over there!' They look. They say, 'You no see something. Twenty pesos each bullet!' Now me not happy. Me think me no more shoot gun."

Garcia paused and his eyes shifted as though seeing something. I waited in anticipation.

"Me see something move in tall grass—" he reenacted his excitement. "Oh! Oh! Me yell, 'Halt!' He no halt; he keep moving. Me yell, 'Halt! You no halt, I shoot!' He no halt. Me yell, 'You no halt, you no answer, I shoot!' He no halt. He no answer. I shoot! Brrraaaappp!

"He say, 'Mooooo!'"

"You shot a cow?" I asked, dumbfounded.

"Si! He no halt. He no answer. I shoot. I kill cow! Sheesh!"

Garcia shrugged, and I lost it. He smiled, and once I had collected myself, he went on.

"They come running. They say, 'You see something move?' I say, 'Si! It move in tall grass!'

They look. They say, 'You kill cow!' They take away my gun! I no like army!"

Eventually, Garcia was put back on guard duty. He told us about that, too.

"The commander, he no like me," he said. "I hate him. He

always tell me I screw up. He put me back on guard. He tell me, 'You no more screw up! You idiot! You stand guard. You no shoot cow! You no shoot air! You watch! You see something move, you shoot!'

"He make me mad. I no like he say, 'You see something move, you shoot!' He get in Jeep—"

"Oh, no," I said, beginning to laugh.

"I see it move!" Garcia continued. "I shoot!"

"Really?" I asked. "You shot the Jeep? With the commander in it?"

"Si! I shoot! I tell him, 'I see move!' Sheesh! He very angry with me."

"Did they make you pay for the Jeep?" I asked. He had told us the price of the cow had come out of his wages.

"They no make me pay for anything," he said. "They put me in jail!"

He wasn't in jail for long that time, but later he did get a long prison sentence, and he explained how that happened, too.

"I go to prison because I shoot uncle," he told us. "I no like uncle. He always make me mad. I shoot him. I shoot him right here—" Garcia slapped himself on the butt. Then with a bewildered look, he shrugged his shoulders and said, "But he die." His expression added, "Can you believe that? Can you believe that they blamed me for him dying?" Then he shrugged his shoulders again and said, "So they put me in prison."

I never figured out how long Garcia spent in the Cuban prison system. But when Castro opened the prisons in 1980 for anyone who was willing to try to go to America, Garcia jumped at the chance. He told a nightmarish tale of his crossing.

"The ride very rough," he recalled, "and many boats too full and people fall off. When people fall off the sharks eat up." Garcia gestured wildly with his hands to show the splashing and eating,

and the look in his eyes expressed the feelings he had felt and
the horror he had witnessed. "Much splashing, much screaming,
much blood. Very scary. Many fights. Many throw somebodies
into the water and the sharks eat. Many mans throw women,
children into water. Is awful, so much screaming. I wish I stay in
Cuba. I no like on water. I no like in boats. But in America, I like.
America is no like Cuba. America is good; Cuba is no good."

I was puzzled about the women and children in the boats,
and when I asked, he explained that Castro had turned the
women prisoners loose also and that many of them had had children in prison and were allowed to take them along.

After he arrived in America, Garcia wound up in St. Louis
working for an electrical contractor. He got married, had his two
kids and seemed to be doing well. I asked him what went wrong
and how he wound up in prison.

"My wife, she find other Cuban," Garcia told me. "I tell her
she no see him; she my wife. She tell me he hire five mans, and
now they kill me, and she marry him. I get gun. I go to see him.
We talk angry in his yard. I tell him, my wife, she say that he hire
five mans to kill me. He say he already pay, now they kill me, he
marry my woman. I shoot him so he die."

I didn't know what to say, but Garcia wasn't finished.

"I go to police station," he continued. "Many mans no look
at me. I go to woman at desk and I say, 'My name is Garcia and
I kill people.' Nothing happen. She no look at me; she busy. No
one look at me, so I say again, 'My name is Garcia and I kill
people.' Nobody look at me. She no look at me. I pull out gun. I
say loudly, 'My name is Garcia, and I kill people!' Sheesh! Now
everybody look at me. All have gun like this—" he dropped into
a crouch, arms extended, right hand cradled in his left, with his
right thumb up and index finger extended.

"Everybody point gun at me!" he said, incredulousness still
in his voice, and once again I was laughing, imagining his bewil-
derment at the scene. "I put gun down—" he mimed gingerly

setting down a gun—"and say, 'No, no, no! I no kill people *now*!
I *already* kill people!' They grab with handcuffs and put me in
jail. I go to trial and judge, he say I go to prison for fifty years. So
I come here and I work for you." Here, he looked at me, grinned
and went on, "And you like to have good Cuban worker who
work hard and keep you out of trouble."

He was right. Alberto Garcia was an unforgettable friend.

Chapter 23

The MSP Gas Chamber

The history books show that forty people died inside the MSP gas chamber. Of those executed, thirty-nine were men and one was a woman. Six were killed in double executions. All but one died from lethal gas; the last died from lethal injection. None died of a heart attack from fright. But I came mighty close.

I first saw the MSP gas chamber on a cold, blowing day in late February 1984 when I toured MSP with my fellow new hires. There were about twenty of us, and we all looked solemnly at the limestone, cube-shaped structure as we filed past it. I found the chamber fascinating and wondered if that meant I had a twisted mind (something most people took for granted), but I later realized that if so, there were a lot of other similarly warped people. Almost every public tour given of the pen would bog down at this place where men and women had been forcefully launched from the here and now into eternity.

I think most of us on that new employee tour were looking at the little stone building, which was built in 1937 with inmate labor, and wondering if it would ever be used again. The death penalty had been on a national hiatus between 1965 and 1975, and in the almost decade since its return to Missouri, there had been no executions, for even as the courts were giving the death sentence, appeals for the convicted men had the system tied up in knots. Allen Sartain, the training officer leading the tour, had pointed out where death row was as we passed by Housing Unit 3. Now I thought of those men, sitting in their cells in the bottom of that building, all hoping their death sentences would be

The MSP gas chamber sometime after the 1988 remodel. A total of forty inmates were executed in the gas chamber between 1937 and 1989.

overturned, but waking up each morning to the realization that most likely, sometime in their future, their appeals would run out. I would later hear some of these inmates joke of taking the big gulp, but something in their eyes belied their bravado.

A couple of months into my career, Bill Wieberg, my boss, called me into his office and told me that it was getting close to an execution date for one of the convicts.

"Of course, the courts will grant an appeal," he said, "but we've still got to get the grass cut and weed-eat around so the big shots coming over to check the place out can be impressed."

I had often driven past the gas chamber, but this was my first opportunity to really look around. What I saw back then was quite different from what visitors see today because of major changes made to the building in the late eighties. Prior to those renovations, the front had two sets of doors with six-inch-high stoops in front of them. Each set had an exterior bar door with a built-in lock and then faded wooden doors with pealing veneer and a hasp with a Yale padlock. On the back of the building were two windows, and the side facing the road had another window. All of these potential exits had strong bars built into the masonry. The top of the building has always had a ragged look because about every other stone was cut with a pointed peak, with the ones between cut off flat.

I walked up a brick sidewalk that ran from the front of the building for about fifty feet before it turned and joined the blacktop road. The sidewalk was wide enough at the building to encompass both front doors and gradually narrowed to about four feet where it met the blacktop. In this walk, oriented to face those entering the building, was a cross, made of concrete and painted white. The cross was about five feet long, three and a half feet wide, with the body of it about ten inches across. The first time I saw it there, the song title "The Way of the Cross Leads Home" came to my mind and established itself there in such a way that ever after, I couldn't see that white cross without thinking of that line.

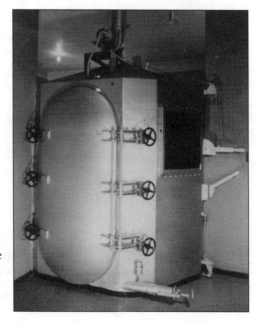

The interior gas chamber in 1987. The pipe sticking out low near the door was used to introduce the neutralizing ammonia as the chamber was being vented. Also visible are the levers for dropping the pill and opening the ceiling pipe vent. Photo from the collection of Mark Schreiber.

The chamber room itself was roughly hexagonal and located in the middle of the building. The viewing room for witnesses and family went around about two-thirds of the chamber room, which had square windows in its walls. Also inside the building were a control room, which had the door to the interior chamber, and two cells. One cell had a bed, a toilet, and a sink. Fastened to the wall above the head of the bed was a crucifix. A heavy door of bars secured this cell. The second cell was used to store the instruments for an execution.

The door to the chamber room was similar to those on a World War II submarine. On the right side of the chamber door were two long handles connected to rods that ran into the chamber. One of these was painted red. When the hatches holding the old "submarine" door were loosened and the door pulled open, two metal chairs were revealed.

It was obvious at first glance that the chairs were not made

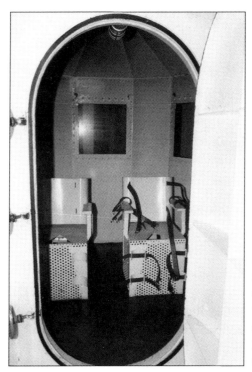

Looking through the interior gas chamber door at the metal chairs where condemned prisoners sat for executions. Photo from the collectin of Mark Schreiber.

for comfort. The metal armrests had slots for leather restraints
and at the chairs' bottoms, similar devices were ready to fasten
the legs. Right under the seat was a little shelf; before an execution, cyanide pills were placed on this shelf and under the shelf
was placed a lead crock filled with sulfuric acid. I thought of
the person who had to reach under the chair and put the pills
in place, all the while knowing what would happen if it slipped
from his fingers and fell into the pot. The actual dropping of the
pills was managed with a lever, workable from the control room
outside the chamber.

As I looked around, morbid fascination tempted me to sit
in the chairs, and when I did, I was surprised to discover that
they sat pretty well. But I can't say I felt comfortable, sitting there
where several people had died. I looked out through the windows
and wondered what it must have been like to know that this view
was your last. I imagined being strapped in and blindfolded and
then listening to the door being shut, the hatches being tightened,
the lever being pulled, the pills sliding off the tilted shelf, the little
"bloop" as it hit the acid. Did it fizz?

I was later told that the gas made a visible mist, and when it
reached the condemned man's face, by a prearranged promise, a
staff witness would tap on the metal chamber so that if the inmate
wanted, he could take a quick deep breath to end it all. Some
involuntarily held their breath to stretch life out for a few more
moments. Once the gas had done its work, a few more minutes
were allowed to pass, then the second lever was pulled to open a
vent in the ceiling and an exhaust fan was activated. Sticking out
near the floor on the outside of the chamber were three-inch pipes
with three small containers mounted to them. The petcocks to
these containers were opened to let ammonia run into the pipes (to
neutralize the gas), and then the end of the pipe was uncapped. The
fan created a draft through the three-inch pipes and the angle created a swirl to rid the chamber of any pockets of gas. This was all
blown out into the air high above the chamber. The tower nearest

the chamber was unmanned during executions, just in case.

As I was sitting in that chair and thinking all manner of macabre thoughts, a sudden clanging reverberated throughout the building. Unsure just what was announcing its presence, I hurtled out of the chair and lunged toward the chamber door. When the phone rang the second time, I recognized the source of the sound but was still a little spooked as to who might be calling. I took a deep breath and answered. It was Wieberg wanting to know how I was getting along. I told him I'd be done in a little while. Something in my voice must have given me away for he asked with a note of concern if I was sure I was all right there by myself. He said I sounded like I had seen a ghost. I said it was just that I hadn't known there was a phone, and the ringing had surprised me.

The next day I was sent back down with paint and gave the chamber a fresh coat inside. While I was painting, a stay of execution was granted.

So the weeds began to grow again, and no one but the occasional tour went inside until another execution date drew near. Then we did it all over again—except for the part about me sitting in there alone in an execution chair. I never did that again.

Chapter 24

Executing an Extreme Makeover

Ralph Sanders was muttering to himself. He was getting louder and angrier and then started swearing at the wall holding his level. We were working in the gas chamber, and I was beginning to wonder if he hadn't disturbed a pocket of old gas. He sure was acting strange, even for Sanders.

It was 1988 and the MSP administration had decided some changes needed to be made to the gas chamber. So Sanders, who was in charge of the carpenter shop, and I were putting paneling along the left wall, just inside the left front door, to cover the old plastered stones. We had two pieces of paneling tacked up, and I was nailing them on when Sanders began his grousing. I kept sneaking glances his direction, and I'd find him taking turns looking at the wall, measuring it, placing his level on it, and growling and cursing, until he finally threw his hammer at a far wall in disgust.

I gave up ignoring him and gently asked if there was a problem. The exact words he snapped at me weren't very nice, but basically, he was upset that the building wasn't level, something I would have taken for granted.

"Just how bad is it?" I asked.

Sanders broke into another tirade concerning the pathetic ancestry of the idiotic builders of the miserable little structure, ending with: "Nine inches! Nine [bleep]-ing inches! How am I supposed to make this job look good now? A [bleep]-ing one-by-six mop-board won't cover the bottom gap!"

I should have known better, but wanting to be helpful, I

suggested dropping each sheet a little bit to make it up. He loudly informed me that we were only going twenty feet, or five sheets, so we'd have to drop each sheet two inches. But I had got him to thinking. The floor trim might just cover the difference, but then the drop ceiling we were going to install would have to be dropped ten inches, too, or even worse, put in ten inches out of level. Sanders mulled it over for a few minutes and then went nuts again, muttering and sputtering that if we did that, then we would be no better than the original idiots.

Now I'm just an old farm boy, and I couldn't see the reasoning behind the remodel anyway. The gas chamber would only be used occasionally, if ever at all, and then not for casual socializing. Who, when attending an execution, is going to be looking around saying, "Oh my, what a nice job someone did paneling this old place! How quaint! I'd just die to have a place like this!"

In the end, Sanders decided to keep the top of the paneling level and cut it off at the bottom to keep a consistent twelve inches between the bottom of the paneling and the floor. Then we added more paneling to the bottom and covered the seam with a piece of trim. This kept the difference in the wall's height hidden in the upper part of the paneling. I think both of us felt satisfied that we had outsmarted the original idiots. (I learned later that one of the inmates who helped build the chamber in the 1930s was eventually executed there. So perhaps the shoddy workmanship was due more to a lack of heart than a lack of brainpower.)

Our remodeling job was more extensive than just adding paneling. We also had to add a wall to divide the viewing room into a witness area—for friends and family of the condemned—and a press witness area. Accomplishing this required extending the wall up and over the top of the slanted, hexagonal metal chamber. It was all compound angles and odd measurements, and for some reason, we weren't allowed to cut, nail, or screw anything into the chamber itself, which I thought was silly. Even if it had leaked a little bit, it would have been in the press area,

and I can't imagine them telling anyone. We even built a minia-
ture three-level bleacher for state and press witnesses to sit on.
The room wasn't nearly big enough for the bleacher, so there was
almost no room for maneuvering.

   We removed the old front doors and the rotting jambs,
and I was rebuilding the jambs by myself one day when I heard
someone calling my name. I went outside and looked around,
but I didn't see anyone in the area. When I turned to go back in, I
heard my name again, and looking towards the clothing factory, I
saw Bulldog, the inmate who had the contents of the kitchen trap
spill on him in 5-C, standing on the other side of the fence. We
had made a bet once, and when he saw how I had tricked him (I
only bet on a sure thing), he refused to pay up. I was delighted for
the chance to taunt him for several months about reneging on a
bet. Once he had gotten out of SMF, I had forgotten him and the
debt. Now he was motioning me to come to the fence. When I
did, he shoved a rolled-up one-dollar bill through to me.

   Now inmates are never allowed to have "green money," and
when I saw what it was, I didn't want to take it for a couple of
reasons. First, I really hadn't wanted to collect on the bet; I just
enjoyed calling him a cheat. And second, and more importantly, I
knew it would be illegal for me to take the dollar and I didn't trust
the giver. I had heard a lot of stories of staff being given marked
money only to be stopped at the front door, searched, and fired.
This guy had once offered me fifty dollars green money to bring
in a toothpaste cap full of marijuana. The only two reasons he
would have done that was to turn me and make me a mule (a staff
person who carried in contraband to the prisoners) or to have me
stopped and fired. When I refused, he laughed it off as a joke.

   Now Bulldog was refusing to take the money back. He
claimed I had made such a fuss over him owing me and now we
were even. But there was no way I was going to carry that dollar
out the front door. I had to get rid of it.

   I suppose I could have written him up, but seeing the part I

State of Missouri

Department of Corrections

and Human Resources

Interoffice Memorandum

Date: 10-20-88

To: ALL EXECUTION CHAMBER PROJECT EMPLOYEES

From: Elmer G. Larkins, Chief Engineer

Subject: JOB WELL DONE!!

I am very grateful to all the employees who assisted in any way on the Execution Chamber Project. You were given a project on short notice. You went ahead and expended great effort to complete it on time. I commend you.

The work done was neat and of high quality. The appearance of the Chamber was highly complimented by the attending officials. Other nice compliments were heard from others about its appearance on the television news.

Again, it is a pleasure to have workers come through for our department. This makes all of us look good before everyone else.

A note of appreciation from Chief Engineer Elmer Larkins to all of the MSP employees who helped with the 1988 remodel of the gas chamber.

had played, I didn't think it right to get him in trouble. If he were setting me up, which I really didn't think was the case, I didn't want prison authorities to come down to the gas chamber looking for the bill and find it. I hadn't nailed the trim up on the inside of the doorjamb yet, so I stuck the dollar in the void between the jamb and the rock and nailed the door trim over it. After MSP was closed, the old doors and jambs were removed and replaced with metal ones. I wonder what those workers thought when they found that dollar. I wonder if they searched for more.

After disposing of the evidence, I washed my hands several times just in case the bill had been marked with ultraviolet dye. I had heard that even when no money was found, dye on a person's hands could be considered proof of guilt. Back in the 1980s, it really was quite a game with some of the inmates and staff to see whom they could set up and get fired. I had heard stories in Corrections Department training classes of staff or inmates dropping drugs in a coat pocket and then having the innocent staff member searched at the front door. We had been taught always to search our pockets before leaving for this very reason, and if we found anything suspicious, we were to report it before we got to the front door.

Not long after Sanders and I finished the remodel, someone far higher up than me decided that we couldn't have the condemned man's family come in through the press area and stumble over the bleachers on their way to their viewing area. No, we must cut a door into the side of the building, through twelve inches of stone. I thought if they tried that, the whole building would fall down, but some of my coworkers went to work cutting, sawing, and chiseling through on the south side of the building next to the road. We ran new electric wire for lights and switches and had it looking pretty good. It was getting on towards summer, and one warm day some of the brass in engineering came to see our marvelous handiwork. As they missed the light switch and stumbled over the bleachers, these big shots began fussing about how warm it was now that the press and family areas were closed off from the front of the building and there was no airflow. Once again we got to work making sure that anyone who came to witness an execution would be comfortable doing it. We built up the back windows with blocks up so high, cut out the bars, and installed two air-conditioners with cages around them to provide security.

A year or so later, it began to look like George "Tiny" Mercer really would be executed. Tiny was the leader of a dope-peddling biker gang. For his birthday, his friends had kidnapped a twenty-two-year-old waitress he admired and given her to him for a present, a gift he was more than willing to share. When they were finished with her, Tiny put his hands around her throat and choked her to death. Later he commented to the buddy who helped him dispose of the corpse that if he had just killed the last [girl] he had raped, he wouldn't be facing his pending rape charges.

I got Tiny's story from the inmates in the plumbing shop. These inmates expressed outrage at the actions of the traitors who turned against Tiny, but several were not particularly upset by what he had done. Some inmates have a strange set of values. Of course, there were some exceptions, but in general, I could expect to hear inmates express moral indignation over someone snitching while defending their right to kill a snitch. Some of the inmates who talked with me didn't feel Tiny had a right to rape the waitress, although many agreed that he would have offended his faithful followers if he hadn't, but several told me that if he felt she was going to snitch him out, he did have an honest right to kill her. Occasionally, in private and in confidence, a convict would tell me that he believed Tiny deserved what it was beginning to look like would happen to him, although even these expressed concern over the state carrying out that function.

At the same time Tiny's appeals seemed to be running out, politicians over at the Capitol were busy trying to change Missouri's form of capital punishment from lethal gas to lethal injection. The main reason for wanting to make this change had little to do with humane execution methods and more to do with the fact that without major renovation, they could not be sure the gas chamber had a good seal, and the executioners and witnesses might all wind up dead.

Then in 1989 a new prison opened at Potosi. The Potosi Correctional Center was set up to carry out the then-state-approved lethal injection, and death row was moved there. There was speculation that if a judge sentenced a condemned man to die in the MSP gas chamber, he might have a legal right to die there. I don't know if that had anything to do with it, but we were told that we must once again modify the gas chamber so that the machinery for the lethal injection could be set up there. The chairs were removed and a gurney installed. In the hall from the front door to the press box, we built a tiny booth against a window so the doctor could monitor the condemned man's vital signs. We also drilled a hole to run monitoring cables in to the gurney, and fastened a mirror to the ceiling so Tiny could see the witnesses and family. We pried out some of the windows and made a couple of frames of one-by-fours to cover the rough metal edges.

I was very upset with the whole operation, as I believed the gas chamber to be an irreplaceable historical building, and I hated to see all of these changes made when Potosi was already set to do lethal injection. I also still believed that the execution would be stopped at the last minute. I was wrong. Tiny Mercer was brought back and kept in "old death row" in receiving (under the administration office area), the prison was locked down, and the execution was carried out, making Tiny the last person put to death in the MSP gas chamber. Within a few days, the implements of execution were moved to Potosi, and all death sentences were carried out there. A few months later the chairs were reinstalled (I was amazed no one had managed to steal them) and the windows were put back in. Sometime after that forty frames were put up on the wall, each with a photo of an executed person, as well as the person's name and date of execution.

So once again the old MSP gas chamber became a place for tours to bog down, people to stare and wonder, and the less timid souls to sit in the death chairs and wonder about a convict's last moments. And everyone I talk to who has seen it mentions that the paneling on the walls sure does look good.

Chapter 25

Doing Time in the Towers

The MSP towers are a familiar symbol of the old institution. Depictions of the towers appear in old newsletters, plaques, T-shirts, and other MSP memorabilia. A popular nickname for MSP was "The Walls," and the towers were a part of the imposing stone perimeter enclosing MSP.

A few of the towers still stand today. The rectangular brick buildings, precariously balanced on top of the round stone towers, were already there when I went to work at the prison, but originally, the towers had round tops that looked a lot like a castle tower in a Robin Hood movie.

The towers were manned 24/7, and there was a standard procedure for officers to gain entrance. First the entering officer would prove his identity to the officer up in the tower. Then the officer in the tower would lower the door key out a window. After unlocking the door, the officer entering would bring the key, still attached to the string, inside and use it to relock the door. The officer would then hang the key next to the locked door and climb up a rickety pipe ladder to a trapdoor that provided admittance to the tower room. The officer being relieved would then climb down, find the key, and reverse the procedure.

Nothing was insulated in the towers except the water pipe, which along with the waste pipe, ran through the tower. There was not much spare room, but officers could stretch their legs on the outside walks. Each tower had a chair, recycled from State Surplus Property and adapted with long homemade legs that raised it up so the officer could sit down and still see the prison

Tower 12 with the
Missouri River
flowing in the back-
ground.

interior. The first tower I ever entered was Tower 3. It was during
my training, and an officer trainee and I were assigned to sit in
Tower 3 with its officer for one long afternoon. Actually, we had to
stand as there was only the one chair, and the officer was careful
not to get up.

Mounted to the ceiling in front of the officer was a two-way
intercom, with the audio piped to all of the towers and the control center. Every fifteen minutes, the officer would lean forward,
push the button, and say "Three-Tower all clear," or the shortened
version, "Three-tower."

Usually after a few hours in the limited confines of these
little square outhouses, people would begin to get bored. Sometimes the voices on the intercom would become imitations of
Daffy Duck, Elmer Fudd, Porky Pig, Walter Brennan, or some

other well-known character. Warden Donald Wyrick frowned on this and would put a quick stop to it when he heard it.

Besides the tall, usually somewhat crippled chair and the speaker, there was a gas heater, the kind often found in homes in the 1970s and 1980s, a combination sink/toilet (such as was used in the housing units), and a gun rack with the weapons and ammunition. About 1990, there began to be small refrigerators in the towers, and later, microwave ovens. No radios, TVs, or reading or writing material were allowed. One former officer explained nightshift tower duty to me this way: "Pull you up a chair to your picture window in the middle of the night and watch an empty street under the streetlights for eight hours, and you'll understand what it's like up in a tower."

Several of the officers who worked nights, especially on the back side of the old prison, told of watching snakes climb the walls. Some people scoffed at this, but I believed it. Growing up on some bluffs overlooking Glaize Creek in Miller County, I saw snakes climb almost straight up what appeared to be a sheared slab of stone. Many evenings, the tower officers fed the night critters that drifted into their lonely domain, making sort of long-distance pets of skunks, groundhogs, stray cats, and other nomadic nocturnal things. Over time these creatures would come on a schedule and keep their benefactors company, and some of the officers would become attached to these pets and would miss them terribly if they stopped keeping their appointments.

Some tower officers would keep count of the number of times they had pushed their intercom button and spoke the number of their tower. Each time brought them closer to ending their miserable banishment from society. It took thirty-two times of listening to lonely voices count up to their tower, then it was their turn, and then they would listen as the count proceeded on up to Tower 15. And then, once again, there was silence. After thirty-two times of this procedure, they listened for the welcome sound of their relief approaching. And if that relief were late in coming, there was anger at every moment of enforced overtime, anger for every moment of fear as the officers dreaded the call from the control center telling them that they would have to pull a double shift and face another thirty-two times of pushing the button and the inevitable struggle to keep their sanity for eight more long hours.

Some officers, after a few weeks of this boredom, began to break under the dismal monotony. To fill the long empty hours, they would do funny things to the tower equipment and their weapons. They would take out fuses, pull apart electric switches, remove screws, and catch bugs or mice and fry them in the microwave (and leave them for the next shift). Sometimes they would dismantle their shotgun. When attempts at reassembling were not successful, they might throw away any leftover parts and no one would know until someone tried to use the weapon. Sometimes a relieving officer would find the casing, gunpowder, and lead from the bullets in little piles.

Those things were inconvenient, but more serious were the times when officers were practicing their lightning-fast quick draw and pistol-spinning reholstering. Occasionally this would result in a bullet hole through a window and an officer's pitiful explanation that he was just checking the gun to ensure it was loaded when it just went off. For some reason it would almost always be the guy who was imitating John Wayne on the intercom that day, although a few times it was someone who just naturally sounded like Barney Fife. This type of behavior was not confined to the night shift either. One of these quick-draw artists shot his own foot and another killed the telephone, both during the daytime.

When I first went to work at MSP, all tower officers were men, but as more and more women were hired, and with the prevailing notion that women shouldn't work inside, more and more of the towers were manned by women. It was not because these women asked for special treatment, but most people who had worked and fought with the hardened felons just did not believe that inside was a place for the gentler sex. Eventually we were all trained that there is no such thing, so it became all right to put women inside. I will confess most of us were surprised at how well it worked.

Much of the tower was made up of single-pane glass, so on sunny summer days, the temperature inside the tower could be anywhere from twenty to forty degrees warmer than outside. In the winter, especially at night, if it was warmer inside than outside, it was not by much. Often in the coldest part of winter, the maintenance person on call for emergencies was in early, hooking up a welder to a tower's frozen water pipes to thaw them and get water up into the tower.

From the outside, the stone towers seemed strong and well-made, but the view from the inside gave a different impression. Mortar was missing, sloppy, or deteriorated, and light came in through at least a million cracks. The stones were not nearly as thick as I had thought and were not uniform in thickness at all. On the outside the joints had been dressed, but the inside mortar joints were left with extra mortar balled up or running down the inside. Tower officers had to look around and wonder if their workplace was about to tumble to the ground.

The fear that a tower might fall down was especially powerful along the railroad tracks where, as the trains went by, the towers would tremble and bits of rock and mortar would rain down from the walls. After I moved up into the engineer's office, and especially after a section of wall fell between Tower 2 and Tower 3, I was asked several times to investigate the possibility that a tower was falling apart. Tower 9 was at the train gate, and the tower itself was solid, but one of the officers was especially concerned that the outside walk was falling apart. The walk was built of poured concrete wrapped with a piece of channel iron that served as both a form and a support. The concrete was cracked and had pieces falling out but nevertheless was sound.

I believe the problem was in part due to the fact that right in front of this tower was the crumbling old chemical plant. A chunk of the plant's foundation had split loose and sunk a few inches, and the old concrete dock was literally falling apart. It was tilted down at about a fifteen-degree angle, and large chunks of concrete had fallen out of it. The funny thing was that it had looked like that when I first started at MSP and as far as I could tell hadn't changed in all the years since. But standing on a walk twenty feet in the air and looking at the crumbling dock started the imagination working. With nothing but that and the recently collapsed wall to think about, it wasn't long until the tower's occupants would be sure the tower was collapsing beneath them. If you have ever sat in your car at a railroad crossing and felt the shake as a train rolled past, then you can imagine what it felt like to officers standing out on the catwalk above the train gate, trying to hang onto their shotguns as they bounced up and down to the rhythm of the passing train cars.

Once I was called to check out Tower 10, as the continual showering of bits and pieces of rock had unnerved the officer stationed there. When she called, she nervously said that the tower was swaying back and forth and was sure to fall at any moment. She asked me to call the control center and have them authorize her to abandon her post. I went out there to look at it and soon realized I had never been in that tower before. Instead of the pipe ladder, it had a magnificent spiral stairway of pie-shaped limestone steps anchored into the wall of the tower, with the inside middle part of each step resting on the one below except for a couple that seemed to defy gravity and stand on thin air with those above still resting on top of them. I determined the tower was still solid and would surely last the rest of the officer's shift. She was not convinced but stuck it out.

The most unusual tower was Tower 15. It sat perched on the administration building, and being on top of a building instead of the old limestone wall was only one of the things that made it different from all of the other towers. Another was that because of its location, it was not manned during the day shift. This had not always been so. In the late 1960s and early 1970s, not only was Tower 15 manned, but there was also another tower, a temporary wooden one, on the front corner of the administration building. During the exercise time for segregated inmates, the officer from Tower 15 would take his shotgun over to this wooden structure. From there he would watch both the roof of the administration building and the wall between there and Tower 1.

Another of the unique things about Tower 15 was how it was reached. Because there was no one in the tower during the day, officers first had to go to the round gate and draw the keys and then recruit someone to go up with them to lock them inside. Often the building's elevator was unavailable, so they had to take the stairs up to the second floor. From there the officers had to find the almost-hidden stairway up to the level of the mailroom and superintendent's conference room. Next, they climbed a ladder that went up to a padlocked trapdoor in the ceiling. Hanging by one arm to this ladder, the officers had to unlock and open the trapdoor. The trick was to hang onto the ladder, climb up one more rung, and keep pushing on the trapdoor until it went over center and would stay open. The occasional mistake in when to turn loose of the trapdoor would result in a banged head. Some managed to avoid this by ducking, only to realize they should have also moved their fingers. Smashed fingers would then cause some people to forget to hang onto the ladder.

Those who avoided these misfortunes found themselves in a twilight-zone maintenance area above the plastered hanging ceiling and the subfloor of the roof. This area was awash with phone lines, electric wires, vent pipes, and other assorted mechanical items and debris. Some was still active, but much had been cut loose or replaced, with the old stuff left behind because no one saw any reason to remove it. From here, there was another short ladder, another trapdoor, and another lock. There was a lightbulb

illuminating the area below the trapdoor, but as it was almost
always burned out, it was little help in finding the right key for
the lock. Officers who were successful in getting through this
second trapdoor (at least this one was counter-balanced) found
themselves in the ancient elevator penthouse.

The antique elevator workings looked to date from the time
of Thomas Edison, and open circuits with large carbon contacts
jumped and sparked each time the elevator was activated. Then
a huge wheel, wrapped with the cable that lifted the car, would
groan and begin to turn. Because the elevator was manually
operated, usually by an inexperienced inmate, stopping the car at
a floor level was managed by jerking the operation handle up and
down until the results were close enough. Watching the mechan-
ics from outside of the cage around the actual electrical panel,
as switches jumped and sparks flew and the huge cable-bound
wheel shuddered one way then the other, was an awesome sight
to behold. It did nothing, however, for my confidence when rid-
ing the elevator, especially when the controller was being jerked
back and forth and the elevator was jumping up and down in
attempted obedience to the commands.

Once the tower officers had made it this far, their accompa-
nying staff members, who were usually the mail runners, handed
up their weapons in a waterproof plastic case, took the keys, and
locked the trapdoor from underneath. I talked to one former
Tower 15 officer who said the first thing he did upon being locked
up there was to go to the edge and look for the softest place to
land if he had to jump down. He said that if a fire broke out in the
administration building, he didn't think anyone would try to get
the doors opened for him.

Now on the flat roof, the officers had to navigate the inevitable pond between them and their tower. This was done by tread-
ing across two-bys that were slimy and slick from long exposure
to the water. The planks were one and a half inches thick, and
the water was usually at least two or three inches deep. When

these slippery walkways suddenly sank underfoot, officers would often lose their balance and have to step, or sometimes fall, into the water. Some of this water had been thickened with several pounds of pigeon droppings, and this helped to cushion a falling body to some extent. Even more dangerous were the times when frost, snow, and ice accumulated on the wooden planks. Several staff were injured because of these conditions. On at least two occasions, the fire department had to be called in to remove the injured officer using a ladder truck.

I have always believed that this obstacle course was not at all a series of unrelated occurrences but were part of a purposefully thought-out plan, so that the tower officers were primed and ready to shoot anyone who gave them half a reason.

Even so, I'd choose what the officer went through to get to Tower 15 over the job of changing the bulbs in floodlights fastened atop the tower. I never knew what this job was like until a few months before the move to the new Jefferson City Correctional Center when a new maintenance man refused to change the bulbs. I went with him to see why. These lights were just below the top of the tower, at least thirty-six inches from the tower wall and sixty feet above the street between D-Dorm and the control center. I asked one of the old-timers how it was done and he explained. "First you get you a ladder up there and an inmate that ain't too scared of heights. Once on top of the tower, you give him the new bulb and slide him over the edge, while a couple more inmates hold his legs. When you get him out far enough, he can undo the lens and change the bulb. When he's done, if he's a pretty good guy, you go ahead and pull him back." I decided instead to get a lift from central equipment depot.

After the move, when I would hear people griping about it being too hot or too cold or too inconvenient to do their jobs at the new institution, I would remember tower officers wearing long underwear, gloves, and heavy coats in the winter, or standing sweat-soaked on the catwalk to escape a sweltering tower in the summer. I would remember square men hanging over the edge of a building or wading knee deep through a sewage spill or crawling through a steam-packed tunnel. And I would wonder just how many of the new prison's employees would be tough enough to last even one day in the conditions that my colleagues and I worked in back behind the old stone walls of MSP.

Chapter 26

The Last Day

In February of 1836, twenty-five years before the start of the Civil War, a battle began in Texas that continues to capture America's imagination. After almost two centuries, we still "Remember the Alamo!" for the patriotic sacrifice made there. While the Alamo was under siege, something else momentous was taking place, although it probably didn't seem all that remarkable at the time. Wilson Eidson, a convicted watch thief, became the first person to enter the Missouri State Penitentiary as an inmate on March 8, 1836.

One hundred and sixty-eight years, six months, and seven days later, my alarm woke me up earlier than usual for what would be another historic day, Wednesday, September 15, 2004, the day that, if all went as planned, the Missouri State Penitentiary would be empty of convicts for the first time since the watch thief had entered its doors.

In spite of all the time I'd had to prepare for that day, I still found I was not ready to say goodbye to the old institution, and as I walked down the sidewalk toward the front door at six a.m., an hour and a half earlier than normal, I could not believe it would be over in a few hours. I went in as usual, climbed the stairs to my office, and made a few calls to ensure we had staff standing by in case they were needed. I let them know they could reach me on the radio. After that, I walked down inside the prison.

In the predawn hour, the upper lawn was brightly lit by security lights, and I saw a couple of trucks and a lot of people gathered in front of Housing Unit 3. Coming out of the unit with their boxes of belongings were inmates. The boxes were being loaded into a truck, and the inmates, each escorted by an officer, were marched up to the control center, down into the receiving area, and then out into a waiting bus. Each one was carefully checked at least three times for proper identification. A helicopter was circling around the prison, and several of the upper echelon of corrections management were together in a group, discussing in hushed, almost reverent tones the operation as it was unfolding. Those attending from the central office included director of the Missouri Department of Corrections Gary Kempker, director of Division of Adult Institutions George Lombardi, and associate director of Division of Adult Institutions Steve Long, while MSP staff in the group included Warden Dave Dormire, Deputy Warden Mark Schreiber, and Deputy Warden Arthur Wood.

I stayed back and listened, not just to the managers' conversation, but to all of the sounds of the morning. I heard orders from officers, subdued responses from the inmates, the distant sound of the helicopter, and the sounds of hundreds of inmates still inside the housing units, not shouting and cursing as I had expected, but quietly gathering their belongings and bringing them down to the front door. Someone asked what the final count was and Schreiber said it was 1,367. I got out my notebook and jotted that down so I would be able to remember.

After a little bit, Schreiber noticed me and came over.

"Well, Larry, my boy," he said, "it's started, and we're here to see it. It won't be long now."

"It's still hard to believe it's happening," I responded.

"Believe it, because today is going to be the end of the line for the old penitentiary. She'll be empty tonight."

I asked a few questions about how certain things were being done and what to expect next, but both of us were thinking much more of the historical significance of what we were witnessing.

Dave Dormire came over and stood by us, but all he said was, "Hello," as he continued to watch the building's lifeblood

drain out in the line of inmates flowing from the doors. I looked
back towards the water tower and saw the early light of dawn;
a few clouds enhanced the beauty of that final sunrise. Seeing
it, I thought of how when I started at the prison, maintenance
had to "stand point," or stand in an assigned spot to watch as the
convicts were released from their housing units for breakfast and
work. Back then everyone was released at once, and the whole
upper lawn would fill with convicts. From my post I had watched
the sun light up the front of Housing Unit 3 several times.

Everyone seemed pleasantly surprised by how well everything was going. The trucks continued to leave as they were filled
up, and others came in to take their places. I spent most of the
day going between the chief engineer's office, Schreiber's office,
and some of the housing units. Then all of the housing units were
empty except 5-A. Schreiber had me trying to keep track of who
had which keys because he felt it was almost certain someone
would try to steal one for a keepsake or possibly to sell online.

A lot of staff members were unashamedly letting their
emotions show that day. Some had spent even more years at
MSP than I had, and I think those who had spent a lot of their
life there were beginning to face the realization that the next day,
they would be reporting for work at the new institution and all
of these familiar sights would be gone from their daily lives. That
day I heard several people reminiscing about experiences they'd
had and people they had known. As I was passing the captain's
office, Schreiber met me and said, "Let's go into Housing Unit 3.
It's empty now. Let's make sure there isn't water running in any
of the cells. We need to be sure that when we leave here these old
buildings are taken care of. We'll need to drain the water and get
all the windows closed up before freezing weather gets here."

We were amazed at how little trash the inmates had left,
although there was some on the floors of the cells and on the
walks. I had found out, just a few months before the move, that
my maternal grandfather had spent two years in MSP back in the

thirties on a charge of statutory rape, and as I walked along looking in the cells, I wondered if he had lived in one of them. I had
searched for any information concerning his time at MSP, but all
I had found was his name and number on a photocopy of his card
in the records office.

As I walked down the walks I remembered inmates I had
worked with, jobs we had done, and staff who had helped me (and
a few who had hindered me). Schreiber had gone one way and
told me I should go another so that we would cover more ground,
but really I think he wanted to be by himself for a few minutes. I
know I did. Later we used the same excuse of checking the place
over to go into A-Hall. Built in 1865 and opened in 1868, it was the
oldest building still standing, and to all MSP staff, it was a special
reminder of the age of the prison. It was the one place we always
wanted to show friends and family members who came for a tour
of the pen.

Housing Unit 3 had not been totally quiet as Schreiber and
I walked around, for there had been others in there also saying
farewell, but A-Hall was absolutely silent. We stopped just inside
the door, momentarily overcome by the stillness and emptiness.
As I slowly looked around, my imagination brought fleeting
ghosts of memories to life. My eyes would see a cell where some
of the guys I had worked with had lived, and for just a moment
they were there again. How many times had I come into this
place in the middle of the night or on a weekend to get whoever
was the current twenty-four-hour plumber? Usually when I got
to his cell, he would ask me to come on in and wait while he got
ready to go. These were men I had worked with for years. I knew
where they came from, if they had families, and as much about
their crimes as they wanted me to know.

Schreiber cleared his throat and told me to take one side
and he'd take the other, and we each climbed a different set of
steps. As I climbed I noticed the worn spots on the steps where
a million feet had hit the same spot for over a hundred years.

We spent quite a while there just wandering and looking. The inmates must have felt something special for the old building, too, for they had left it nearly spotless, many of them even making up their beds and some leaving notes.

Late in the day as I was still checking various buildings and ensuring that water was off, toilets weren't running, and doors were closed and locked, I overheard someone say they were about to load up the last few inmates. There had been some kind of hang-up in Housing Unit 5, but now the inmates there were ready to go. I walked over, noticing that no one was locking the gates anymore. I stood by the front of the building as the last inmates, secured with leg-irons and handcuffs, were loaded on the bus, and then I watched as the bus drove down the hill.

Eventually I wound up in Schreiber's office. I was one of the few still officially on duty in what we were assuming was the now-empty Missouri State Penitentiary. The towers and control center were still manned and would be until the count cleared at the new Jefferson City Correctional Center. We had to know that nobody had managed to hide out and avoid getting on the bus. The counts had been careful, and each inmate had been accounted for, but we couldn't afford to be wrong. We had been notified when the last bus had unloaded and the inmates were locked down that we could expect the count to clear in just a few minutes. The first count at the Jefferson City Correctional Center was wrong, off by several. Schreiber said it was a bad count, but that we would have had to worry if they had only been off by one or two. They were in the process of recounting and told us to expect the count to clear in about thirty minutes. An hour went by, and we finally heard that the count was wrong again but was a lot closer this time. After what seemed like an eternity but was more like another hour, we got word that the count had cleared. None of us seemed to want to leave, and then the announcement came over the radio from the control center stating that MSP was now secured, all towers could empty their posts, and all watches

State of Missouri
Department of Corrections
Inter-Office Communication

MISSOURI STATE PENITENTIARY

Date: September 15, 2004

TO: Ron Arney MSI

FROM: Larry E. Neal PME II

SUBJECT: Appreciation

I want to express my appreciation for the work that you have done these last few months and to apologize for missing you when I was doing the other letters this morning. The upside of that is that you are receiving what is most likely the last IOC to be written in the Missouri State Penitentiary as it is now 4:13 PM, and the last busload of offenders is at or leaving the traingate now. I am sure you have wondered what you got yourself into when you came to work here and found yourself to be one of the last maintenance personnel to keep the place running. You, along with Bill and Charley, have done a tremendous job and I hope that you know that it has been appreciated.

Thank you for a job well done.

. C: Steve Kroner
File

The last known interoffice communication from MSP, written on the day the institution closed. It is a note of appreciation from Neal, then a plant maintenance engineer, to a maintenance supervisor.

were to stand down. Then we heard, "The Missouri State Penitentiary is now officially closed."

No one said anything. We looked at one another, and then one by one, we quietly drifted out.

A strange feeling hit me at the front door, where I found both slider doors open. It was the first time I had not had to wait for one or the other to open. The sound of that slider banging closed behind me the first day I had walked in had almost caused me to turn around and walk out. I never would've believed then that one day, I'd have the opposite internal struggle, that I'd find leaving so impossibly hard.

Stepping outside, I looked down the street and saw the officer coming out of Tower 1. Last time. There had been a lot of last times that day.

Larry Neal walking from the upper yard toward M&M, the MSP maintenance shop, in 2006, two years after MSP closed. Photo by by L. G. Patterson of Recess Inc.

There was still a lot to be done to close and secure all of the property, and I would be back several times in the next few weeks, but I didn't know it then. I felt as if I had just watched an old friend breathe her last as I walked down the street to my car. It was parked across the street from Tower 4, in almost the very same place I had parked on my first day.

As I got in my car and looked though its windows at the old wall and towers, I thought of a story I had written a few months earlier for the personnel newsletter, in which I encouraged my fellow staff members to appreciate the history they were witnessing. "One day this year," I wrote, "the Missouri State Penitentiary as such will cease to exist. It will become the 'historical site of the original prison,' and most of it will be torn down. Parts of it will be kept as a curiosity, a museum of the past, a place where dangerous criminals were once incarcerated to protect society. People will view the cold empty buildings and wonder about the people who were willing to work in such a place. We will be the people that they will try to picture in their minds.

"We have taken our place upon the stage," I continued, "and played out our part, and now that part of the story of our lives is intertwined with the story of every other person who has worked, or lived in this place. Whether you realize it or not, you have a story to tell. . . . Someday you might drive by whatever remains of these old walls with your grandkid, and you can say, 'That's where the old Missouri State Penitentiary was. And I worked in there back when it was full of convicts.'"